THE
DEPRESSION
TOOLKIT

Quick Relief to Improve Mood, Increase Motivation & Feel Better Now

WILLIAM J. KNAUS, EDD • ALEX KORB, PHD
PATRICIA J. ROBINSON, PHD
LISA M. SCHAB, LCSW • KIRK D. STROSAHL, PHD

New Harbinger Publications, Inc.

Publisher's Note

Distributed in Canada by Raincoast Books

NEW HARBINGER PUBLICATIONS is a registered trademark of New Harbinger Publications, Inc.

Copyright © 2022 by Alex Korb, William J. Knaus, Patricia J. Robinson,
Lisa Schab, and Kirk Strosahl
New Harbinger Publications, Inc.
5674 Shattuck Avenue
Oakland, CA 94609
www.newharbinger.com

Cover design by Amy Shoup; Acquired by Ryan Buresh; Edited by Joyce Wu

---

Library of Congress Cataloging-in-Publication Data

Names: Knaus, William J., author. | Korb, Alex, PhD, author. | Robinson, Patricia J.,
   author. | Schab, Lisa M., author. | Strosahl, Kirk, 1950- author.
Title: The depression toolkit : quick relief to improve mood, increase motivation,
   and feel better now / by William J. Knaus, Alex Korb, Patricia J. Robinson,
   Lisa M. Schab, Kirk D. Strosahl.
Description: Oakland, CA : New Harbinger Publications, [2022] | Includes biblio-
   graphical references.
Identifiers: LCCN 2021039777 | ISBN 9781648480065 (trade paperback)
Subjects: LCSH: Depression, Mental.
Classification: LCC RC537 .K572 2022 | DDC 616.85/27--dc23
LC record available at https://lccn.loc.gov/2021039777

Printed in the United States of America

23   22   21

10   9   8   7   6   5   4   3   2   1   First Printing

CONTENTS

Part 3: Beat Hopelessness and Low Motivation

Part 4: Make Easy Habit Changes That You'll Thank Yourself for Later

Part 5: Deal with the Tough Stuff

INTRODUCTION

These are extreme and uncertain times. From natural disasters to downsizing and automation to global pandemics that previously seemed unimaginable—not to mention political division about all of the above—we have more than enough to feel sad, hopeless, and down about.

When picking up this book, you likely sought relief from the burden of negative thoughts, obsessive thinking about things that won't get any better, or the weighted-down, "there's no point" feeling that depression leaves in your body. This book will help you feel better, but it's important to know that your feelings are valid. These days, it can be hard *not* to feel that nothing you can do will change either the world or your feelings, or that nothing will get better. These concerns are also valid, and this book is here to help you deal with them in a productive way.

As for the bad days...we believe that this book can help. The techniques in this mental health toolkit can give you a welcome respite from depressive thoughts and low mood so that you can focus on feeling better in the here and now.

In this short book, we have compiled the easiest and most effective depression-reducing exercises, techniques, and practices from top mental health experts. All these techniques come from evidence-based treatments. By "evidence-based," we mean that the tools in this book have been tested and approved in research labs all over the world and have worked for decades with many clients.

Perhaps you have heard about cognitive behavioral therapy, acceptance and commitment therapy, or neuroscience. If you have, then you might have a sense of how this book will help you. If you haven't, don't worry. Knowing these therapies is not important to get the most out of this book. Here, we want to focus on improving your mood, helping you get a better understanding of your thoughts, and making sure you are living in accordance with what really matters to you. If you are already interested in these therapies, or if this book inspires your curiosity, you can explore these topics in any number of other books from New Harbinger.

This book starts by teaching you techniques to reduce the kind of spiraling thinking that depression presents before you start the more difficult work of managing how you feel. If you're able, we recommend working through the book from beginning to end, because it's easier to work on your depression once you've established a baseline of calm, or nonreactivity.

This book is also designed to get you what you need when you need it, so you don't have to try all of the techniques if you already know what works for you. Similarly, if you find that the mindfulness exercise, for example, works well for you, simply make it a habit and move on to the next part. All the techniques in this book can be used as needed and on demand. They are flexible enough to work with any kind of depression, thought, or feeling, so feel free to jump in and out. Perhaps leaving the book on the coffee table—or somewhere else where it's readily available—can help it to deliver relief when you need it.

As you move through the book, try to bring whatever amount of playfulness you can to these exercises and techniques. We know that it can be tough when you're struggling. But do your best. It's important to keep an open mind. That said, if something doesn't feel like it's working for you, drop it and move on to something else. In these pages, you are the priority.

These times are truly distressing, but finding a moment to take care of your mental health doesn't have to be. With that…let's take a deep breath and get started.

PART 1

FIND REFUGE FROM NEGATIVE THOUGHTS

1: CHOOSE POSITIVE THOUGHTS

What to Know

The way people think directly affects their moods. One way to combat feelings of depression is by practicing positive thinking instead of negative thinking.

Cameron had just gotten home from work, and he was feeling depressed. His partner noticed that he looked sad and asked him how his day had gone. Cameron said that something upsetting had happened: he had received an award for his performance over the last quarter.

His partner asked why that made him feel upset. Cameron said that he didn't think he deserved the award, and now he would feel pressured to live up to it. Then Cameron said that the office was giving a party for him. His partner said that sounded like fun, but Cameron told her that the party would be at a restaurant that held bad memories for him. It was the last place he had been with his ex-girlfriend before she broke up with him.

When Cameron's partner suggested he try to go anyway, Cameron told her there was more. The director was presenting him with a gift certificate to a music store at a nearby mall. It seemed like it was an appropriate and generous gift, but Cameron reminded her that he hated going to the mall because it was so noisy and crowded.

Cameron's partner finally told him, "Situations aren't negative or positive in and of themselves. It's how we choose to think about situations that makes us feel happy or depressed. You're feeling depressed because you are choosing to think the most negative possible thoughts about everything. What if you tried to think more realistic thoughts, and to look for the positives whenever you can? You might feel much better." They talked about it together, and Cameron decided he'd try to change some of his dark thoughts.

The negative thought *I don't deserve the award; now I'll feel pressured to live up to it* became the positive thought *I trust the director's judgment. If he chose me for the award, I must deserve it.*

The negative thought *I will feel terrible going to that restaurant because of the bad memories* became the positive thought *I can't avoid that restaurant forever. This is a good chance to create new, positive memories there.*

And Cameron found that when he changed his thoughts from negative to positive, his mood changed, too.

What to Do

Changing our thoughts to change our feelings is a simple idea, but it's not always easy to do. Some life situations are very difficult, and it's hard to think about them in a positive way.

Pick a situation from the list below, and then write a negative statement that could make someone feel depressed about it, followed by a positive statement that could make someone feel happy about it.

- Being youngest in the family

- Being very tall

- Going to a party

- Getting a new puppy

- Being elected class president

- School closing because of bad weather

- Being the first one to give your oral report

- Being an only child

- Being last in line for the roller coaster

- Moving to a new town

Next, think of something that happened to you in the last week that you felt happy about.

Remember as many of the positive thoughts you told yourself to feel happy about this as you can.

Now, think of two or more negative thoughts that could have made you feel depressed about the event.

Next, flip the order. Think of something that happened to you in the last week that you felt depressed about. List a few of the negative thoughts you told yourself that made you feel depressed about this in your head.

Now, find a blank piece of paper or open the notes app on your phone and write two or more positive thoughts that could have made you feel happy about the event.

Remember that you are the only one who can choose your thoughts!

2: THE BREATH OF LIFE

What to Know

The breath is the center of your being. It controls not only your respiration, but also your heart rate, brain waves, skin temperature, and a host of other basic biological functions. Coincidentally, deep, regular breathing has been shown to help down-regulate the brain's fight-or-flight system, which is a source of negative energy for the reactive mind—the part of our mind in which our thoughts and emotions can run wild. So, what we call belly breathing actually optimizes the neural pathways responsible for calming the nervous system and producing a state of what we can call "wise mind": a state of mind in which we can use our rational and emotional faculties flexibly to act in the ways that serve us and bring us ease.

Indeed, the Buddhist term for this type of deep breathing practice is *pranayama,* which literally means "the breath of life." How powerful is pranayama? Research shows that people who can be aware of each breath report improved ability to pay attention in real life, report less daydreaming and mind wandering, and experience more positive moods with lessened depression (Levenson, Stohl, Kindy, and Davidson 2014). The benefits of this breathing practice were observed to occur within two weeks of starting!

What to Do

Find a comfortable place to sit and make sure the clothes you're wearing aren't tight so that you can breathe very deeply. Get your body in a comfortable position and close your eyes for a few minutes. Begin by focusing your attention on your breath. Just notice your breathing for a while without trying to change it in any way. Take your time to get present with your breathing. This is the present moment in your life, and there is no reason to rush through it. Just allow yourself to breathe in and out however your body wants to do it.

Now, imagine there's a balloon in your belly that you want to fill with the air you inhale. As you breathe in very slowly and deeply, you're filling the balloon in your belly. When you are filling the balloon, you will notice that your belly is pushing out and down. When the balloon is full, pause for a second and then gradually let the air flow out of the balloon. When you empty the balloon, you will notice that your belly pulls in and up slightly. As you inhale and exhale, your chest and shoulders should remain almost still. If you notice that your chest and shoulders are rising and falling, try to send your breath into your belly and allow your chest and shoulders to remain still and relaxed.

Now, as you inhale, purse your lips and breathe in through your nose. Notice the sensation of the air coming up through your nose and down into the balloon in your belly. Imagine this flow of air as an upside-down umbrella handle. You start at the crooked end of the umbrella handle, then bring your breath up into your nose and down the handle into the balloon. As you exhale, open your lips and reverse the direction of your breath along the umbrella handle. Your breath leaves the balloon, comes up the long, straight handle, then travels over the arch and out of your mouth. Now, as you continue to focus only on your breathing, notice any sensations you experience as the breath goes in through your nose and back down to your belly. Do you notice the temperature of the air as you bring it in? What does it feel like as it goes through your nose? And as you exhale, does the air seem warm or moist as it passes your lips? If you notice your attention shifting away from breathing, gently redirect it to what you have come here to do. Continue to fill and empty the balloon for five minutes.

More to Do

What experiences did you have when you practiced this basic breathing exercise? Were you able to consciously fill the balloon in your belly? Did you notice your mind wandering while you were breathing? Were you able to bring your attention and focus back to the task at hand?

Don't get frustrated if this exercise is difficult at first. The simplest things, like breathing, can seem like a big mental task when your reactive mind tries to get in the way. We strongly recommend that you practice this or another breathing exercise that you like at least once a day—even better, several times a day, morning, noon, and night. The more you practice, the more accustomed you will become to using the present moment as an anchor on your life journey.

3: THE GIFT OF THE MOMENT

What to Know

Some people have a habit of looking into the future with a negative focus. They spend a lot of time predicting negative outcomes, missing the positive things that are happening to them in the present moment. This contributes to their feeling depressed. Keeping an equal amount of mental focus on the positive qualities of the present can help you combat depressive feelings.

Elana worked hard, had friends and a family who loved her, and was healthy. But Elana felt more and more depressed every day. She didn't seem to get much pleasure from anything she did, and she was spending more time at home alone with her computer than out with her friends. Elana's mother was worried and took her to the doctor for a checkup.

The doctor could find nothing physically wrong with Elana, so she asked how her life was going. Elana said that she felt like everything she did was useless. She spent most of her time working to advance her career and make more money. She figured she would have to work even harder in a future job to pay all of her bills and save enough money to retire. And then she figured that after all that hard work, she would probably have a heart attack and die. What was the point of doing anything at all?

You can see how Elana was focusing on the negative. The thoughts Elana was having probably reflected a distorted reality. They also made it harder for her to deal with the way she felt, for instance, by doing more that made her feel good and seeing people who cared for her.

If you struggle with a negative focus, what can you do to help yourself? Try looking for the positive—the gifts that are present in each moment we're alive.

What to Do

- **Keep a gratitude list.** Every day, write down at least five things that you are grateful for. You can choose anything, from liking the color of your bedroom to laughing with a friend to getting a good grade. Hang the list where you can see it all the time.

- **Plan activities you like to do.** Make a list of daily and weekly activities that you enjoy: listening to music, playing with your dog, watching movies, swimming, or anything else that makes you happy. Plan them into your schedule, so that you have something positive to do every day.

- **Practice focusing on what you are doing in the present moment.** If you are eating ice cream, really pay attention to its taste, texture, and color, and to how much you are enjoying it. If you are riding a bike, pay full attention to the experience—the feel of the path, the freedom of the wind in your hair, and the fun of the ride.

- **Stop negative focus on the future.** If you notice yourself thinking negative thoughts, tell yourself, *Stop!* and turn your mind to something positive in the present instead.

For the next week, practice the above suggestions in your own life. After seven days, your gratitude list should have a lot of items. Pick out the pleasurable activities that were most realistic for you to do daily and weekly and most genuinely enjoyable to do. As you go about your week, reserve a time to reflect on what it was like trying to shift your focus this week. Evaluate which seems more natural to you—focusing on the present moment or thinking about the future—and why.

4: FIND A POSITIVE METAPHOR

What to Know

One of the most consistent findings in brain research on depression is that depression is associated with less activity in the right frontal lobes (Heller and Nitschke 1997). This is the part of your brain that does the heavy lifting for creativity, curiosity, imagination, and play. It gets activated by listening to music or being absorbed in art. It's a playful and spontaneous part of your brain that basically goes dormant when you're depressed. But activating it can help combat low mood. By creating positive metaphors, using similes, and writing poetry for example, you can put this right side of your brain to use. The effect is kind of like turning on a light in the other room and realizing how nice it might be to stay there for a little bit. By engaging in activities that light up this part of your brain, you spend small amounts of time with the intuition and artistic abilities that can help you process your thoughts and feelings in a constructive and helpful way.

A metaphor is a figurative comparison, such as "life is a cornucopia." There are many historical metaphors for depression and low mood. Winston Churchill, for instance, said his depressed mood was a black dog that followed him. "A prison beneath jimsonweed" calls forth another depressing image. "Trapped in a tomb" captures another.

But metaphors can also point to exits from depression. For example, when the winds of depression descend upon you, you can adjust your sails to move yourself toward safe harbors. You can also think of bats of depression that fly in the night, which you can dispatch by the light. Now, find an action that gets you to the harbor and the bats ducking for cover.

What to Do

1. Use scratch paper or your notes app to write down the metaphor for depression that works best for you—that feels vivid and true to your experience—and like something you can intervene in.

2. Now, just below that, create a positive action metaphor that contrasts with your depression metaphor—the same way that, say, you can adjust a sail when the winds of depression threaten to blow you astray.

More to Do

If you'd like to expand on this exercise, you could portray your depression through poetry. The rhymes could describe misery. You could also write a poem that shows how to move away from depression. Think creatively.

The philosopher Aristotle said, about twenty-five hundred years ago, that life and events have a beginning, a middle, and an end. So does depression. And by learning what to do and applying what you know, you can bring it to its end sooner. Use your imagination as constructively as you can. Taking the tiniest step signals that you have started the process of making positive personal changes and disentangling yourself from the web of depression: a complex, sticky place where few would voluntarily choose to go or stay.

5: DEPRESSIVE THOUGHTS AS HYPOTHESES

What to Know

Often, when we're depressed, we think thoughts like *I'll stay depressed forever.* What if you treated this thought as a hypothesis? Maybe it's not a statement of truth but rather a proposition that you can test. And with such propositions, your goal is to experiment so you can learn which ones hold up and which don't.

So, the next time you feel stuck in a depressive line of thought, reframe the issue from a depressive dogma to a hypothesis you can test.

What to Do

Use the following framework to transform your depressive thoughts into fluid hypotheses.

Depressive Thought: *I can't do anything right.* → **Hypothesis:**
I hypothesize that whatever I undertake will turn out badly.

Depressive Thought: *I will never stop feeling depressed.* → **Hypothesis:**
I hypothesize that depression will last forever.

Now, you are in a good position to compare your hypotheses to actual outcomes. Give yourself a moment to focus on a depressive thought you've had lately. Turn it into a hypothesis. Focus on the words, particularly ones like "whatever I do" and "forever." Test the hypotheses out in your mind. Can they be proven right? What would have to happen to prove them correct? Most likely the hypotheses are too rigid or long ranging—you'd have to spend lifetimes getting enough data to prove them correct. In flipping depressive thoughts into statements for which we need to find proof, we find the fictions at the heart of our thinking. Even just hinting at the shaky ground these thoughts are on helps strip the power from our thoughts.

6: DETECT DEPRESSIVE DECEPTIONS

What to Know

People normally don't consciously go out of their way to fool themselves. Rather, they have some self-deceiving habits of mind.

When you are depressed, how do you know when you are deceiv-
ing yourself? One way to check is to thoroughly examine a thought
using an easy-to-replicate process called the Plausibility Checklist. In
this process you are going to:

1. State the suspected depressive idea.

2. Ask yourself five plausibility questions.

3. Answer each question with a simple yes or no.

4. Give your reason for your conclusion.

For example, let's say your friend Bart borrowed money from you
under the false pretense that he needed a temporary loan to keep his
business going. Instead, he gambled the money away in an ill-fated
hope that he could make enough money to pay his business expenses
and pay you back. Now he can't and won't repay you.

Depressive idea: *I'll never get over Bart's betrayal and will suffer forever.*

Here are five plausibility questions you might ask yourself to challenge the depressive idea:

1. **Does this idea seem plausible?**
    There is a partial truth here. Betrayals will negatively affect
    most reasonable people. Suffering a dollar loss from deception
    can be emotionally rattling. However, saying you will suffer
    forever is jumping to a conclusion.

2. **Does the idea fit with expected life experiences?**
   Yes. Betrayals are inevitable in life.

3. **Is this idea consistent with known facts or probabilities?**
   It's reasonable to predict that you might lose the money you loan a gambler. It's less reasonable to predict that you will stay burdened with the results of a betrayal forever. That would be like making a magical leap from what is remotely possible to what is certain.

4. **Is there an advantage to believing this idea?**
   There is no healthy advantage in believing that you will suffer forever.

5. **Would knowledgeable and rational people agree with this idea?**
   Most would agree that Bart's deception was costly. Feeling bad about the betrayal and loss is reasonable. Distrusting Bart now makes sense. There is no requirement to overgeneralize and expect to suffer forever.

All in all, the idea of suffering forever doesn't fit with experience. Depression lifts. Dollars lost can sometimes be recovered.

What to Do

The plausibility checklist helps you to get a perspective on your own thinking and to eliminate self-deceptions. Try it and see. Think of your latest depressive thought:

☐ State the suspected depressive idea.

☐ Ask yourself five plausibility questions:

   1. Does this idea seem plausible?

2. Does the idea fit with expected life experiences?

3. Is this idea consistent with known facts or probabilities?

4. Is there an advantage to believing this idea?

5. Would knowledgeable and rational people agree with this idea?

☐ Answer each question with a simple yes or no.

☐ Give your reason for your conclusion.

Recognizing depressive thoughts, categorizing them, and questioning their validity is a remedy for depression with a big side benefit. You may find yourself increasingly alert to the overgeneralizations, biases, and distorted thinking of others, like those of well-known news commentators and political pundits who routinely skirt issues and twist reality through overgeneralizations and other forms of cognitive distortions. However, the most important change is that you may recognize that there are many ways to view and categorize negative thinking, and you can choose how you go about doing this.

7: WHAT TIMELINE ARE YOU ON?

What to Know

To help you learn how to get into the present moment and stay there as much as possible, let's do an exercise to find out what time zone—past, present, or future—you are inhabiting at the moment. Think of time as a continuum ranging from your most remote memories of early childhood to future projections that go all the way to the moment of your death—and possibly beyond. There is nothing good or bad about where your mind goes, so try not to think in those terms. The goal is simply to get to know your reactive mind and better understand its preferences.

What to Do

In the time continuum graphic, the present moment is the middle of the line. Go ahead and place your index finger there, and then read on.

Timeline				
Distant Past	Recent Past	Present Moment	Near Future	Distant Future

The first step of this exercise is to close your eyes, take some deep, cleansing breaths, and put the cares and concerns of the day to one side as best you can. Just try to clear your mind so that you can stay in the present moment for a few minutes. If you notice your mind wandering, simply notice that it's wandering, and begin to move your finger. If your mind is drifting into the past, slide your finger to the left. For a distant childhood memory, your finger would go all the way to the left; more recent memories would bring you finger closer to the present-moment notch on the timeline. If your mind heads way into the future—say imagining your life at a very old age—your finger would go all the way to the right; a more immediate thought of the future, like what present to buy for a friend's birthday next month, would move your finger toward a position just right of the center of the timeline.

Just let your mind drift in whatever direction it wants to go, without forcing it to change course. See if you can simply notice where your mind is on the timeline at any moment in time. If you suddenly realize you got pulled out of this exercise, just recall the time orientation of the last thought or memory you had. Gently put your attention back onto just noticing where your mind is traveling when you give it free reign.

More to Do

When you are ready to come back to your normal waking state, take some time to reflect on the following questions:

- How often did you find yourself in the present moment (for example, noticing the sensation of your finger on the paper, or your breathing)?

- Where on the timeline did your mind tend to take you when you left the present moment?

- Did particular thoughts, feelings, memories, or sensations lure you out of the present moment more than once or on an ongoing basis?

Did you find it hard to stay in the present moment during this exercise? For most people, this two- or three-minute exercise seems like ten! In modern society, we hardly ever take the time to just sit and explore the present moment. Did you have the experience of suddenly realizing you weren't in the present moment at all, almost like you woke up and found yourself somewhere else? We all do. The process of fusing with our thoughts, emotions, and memories happens automatically and often. This is why practice and intention are fundamental to shifting attention back to the present moment.

8: IDENTIFY STICKY THOUGHTS

What to Do

Take some time to think about past and present situations in which your reactive mind may have tricked you into attaching to a sticky thought. Using a piece of paper, write down each of these destructive messages as accurately as you can. Use the format below.

- My negative personal qualities and shortcomings:

- What I should be thinking, feeling, or remembering:

- What will happen if I address a painful personal problem:

- Comparing how I feel right now to how I should be feeling:

- How other people's lives are going compared with mine:

- Mistakes I've made and how they'll affect my future:

- What other people think about me and my issues:

- Seeking help from a spouse, partner, or friends:

More to Do

What did you discover as you worked through this exercise? Did certain themes reappear in various categories? Did you sometimes argue with yourself that certain sticky thoughts might represent the truth? This is what sticky thoughts do; they get you to swallow them, and then you're forced to struggle with them once you've been hooked. The more you struggle, the deeper the hook sets.

In order to take power away from these sticky thoughts, we need to see them for what they are. Now, look back at your list. Beside each thought, give it a nickname. For instance, give the *How I should be feeling* thought a nickname—"The Better Options Trap," for example. And do that for each thought. By naming them, you can help yourself notice when they are getting sticky and remind yourself, *That's just my Better Options Trap.*

9: THANK YOUR MIND

What to Know

Since you can't keep your mind from thinking, feeling, remembering, and sensing, learning how to distance yourself from your mind when it's provoking you is important. Expressing gratitude to your mind—out loud—for the intelligence it's giving you is one sure way to create a more workable relationship between you and your mind. This allows you to respond in a voluntary, intentional way to your reactive mind, rather than falling for the content of sticky thoughts. This strategy also requires you to do some more naming.

What to Do

Here's how it works: when you notice an unpleasant mental event unfolding, simply say, *Thank you, mind, for giving me the* [thought, feeling, memory, sensation] *called* [describe the sticky thought]. You can use the nicknames you generated in the last exercise, if you like. Try to get in the habit of doing this any time your reactive mind gives you a sticky thought of any kind. In Helen's case, she thanked her mind in the following ways:

- *Thank you, mind, for giving me the thought called* fat, ugly girl.

- *Thank you, mind, for giving me the thought called* You come from a messed-up past.

- *Thank you, mind, for giving me the memory called* My drunk dad tells me I'm disgusting.

- *Thank you, mind, for giving me the feelings called* sad and scared.

- *Thank you, mind, for giving me the thought* You are a coward.

- *Thank you, mind, for giving me the feeling called* loneliness.

By simply describing sticky thoughts and creating nicknames for them, you're building skills that will allow you to relate to your reactive mind in a different way. You don't have to mindlessly follow what your mind tells you to do. You are the human being; the mind is at your service, not vice versa. Learning to hold that detached posture when your reactive mind is yakking at you is an essential step toward moving through depression and reclaiming your life.

10: STICKY MOMENTS

What to Do

This exercise is particularly useful when you have been through an emotionally charged interaction, event, or situation in which you struggled to remain detached. Get a stack of sticky notes and, thinking back through the situation, try to identify the following:

- Thoughts that got me

- Feelings that got me

- Memories that got me

- Bodily sensations that got me

- Urges that got me

Write each of these items down on a sticky note, one item per note. After you've finished writing an item down, peel the note off the pad, read it out loud, and then attach the sticky note to your clothing. Keep doing this until you've worked your way through the entire assortment of experiences that got you. After all the notes are stuck to your clothing, look in a mirror and quietly move your eyes from note to note. Read what each note says; allow whatever shows up inside of you to be there without trying to change, control, or eliminate it.

More to Do

As you went through this exercise, did you notice if there were certain types of sticky experiences that kept hooking you, sometimes long after the original situation had ended? Did you find that you intended to just read the sticky thought out loud and do nothing at all, only to realize that all of a sudden you were off and running with your reactive mind?

As we mentioned earlier, not all sticky experiences are created equal; some are much harder than others to detach from and let go of. These are often deep-seated themes that might have played out in your life a number of times, so if you ran into them, make a mental note of what they are, because you will be running into them again as you heal. Remember: we all have our skeletons in the closet, so don't get down on yourself if you notice one of yours has shown up.

11: HACK YOUR BRAIN CHEMICALS

What to Know

Picture the flight map in the back of an in-flight magazine showing all the cities an airline flies to and from. That'll give you a pretty good idea of the organization of a neurotransmitter system, which simply means all the neurons that release or react to a particular neurotransmitter. Your brain relies on numerous neurotransmitter systems for different types of processing, and they contribute to depression in different ways.

In the 1960s, depression was thought to be a matter of having too little of the neurotransmitter norepinephrine. Then, a few years later, the theory changed to a deficiency of serotonin. We now know it's much more complicated than that. Sure, serotonin and norepinephrine are involved, but so are dopamine and numerous other neurochemicals. Ultimately, a whole bunch of neurotransmitter systems influence—and are influenced by—depression. On the bright side, there are a number of ways we, too, can influence and hack this system—starting right away.

What to Do

Within the next hour, try one of the following brain hacks:

- Go out in the sunlight. Bright sunlight helps boost the production of serotonin. It also improves the release of melatonin, which helps you get a better night's sleep. So, if you're stuck inside, make an effort to go outside for at least a few minutes in the middle of the day. Go for a walk, listen to some music, or just soak in the sun.

- Think of happy memories. Happy memories boost serotonin. Try to think of one happy memory. You can also try this right before you go to sleep—write it in a journal or just reflect on it.

12: FIND A BUMMER BUDDY

What to Know

Depression often makes you want to be alone, but in fact, spending time with friends and relatives eases a depressed mood. Surprisingly, the support of friends and family even improves the effects of antidepressant medications. People who have more social support before they start taking medication are more likely to experience a reduction in their symptoms and also more likely to feel better. In addition, the same study showed that as people's symptoms improved, their social support did too (Joseph et al. 2011). So, being social helps you get better, and getting better helps you be more social—a healthy upward spiral.

What to Do

- Do an activity with a friend. Often when you're depressed, you don't feel like talking. Try an activity in which you can engage with someone but won't feel pressured to talk. Go see a movie or play a board game. You won't feel forced to talk about your depression if you don't want to, but there will be opportunities to open up if you feel like it.

- Even talking to strangers can help. One study in Chicago paid bus and train commuters to either strike up a conversation with a stranger or just sit quietly (Epley, Schroeder, and Waytz 2013). The results showed that talking with a stranger led to better moods. In fact, while most people were worried that talking with a stranger would be unpleasant, after doing so, they actually had a happier commute. So, try talking to the person next to you on a plane or in line with you at a coffee shop. Sure, you might be apprehensive, but chances are, it'll be a positive experience.

PART 2

GET UNSTUCK WHEN YOU'RE DOWN

13: LEARN TO LET GO

What to Know

When people mentally hold on to problems, they think about them over and over, worrying about what will happen and picturing the worst possible outcome. This process can cause someone to feel depressed. Learning to mentally let go of problems can help you let go of depression as well.

Marc and Kevin were twins. They were alike in many ways; their hair color and the turn of their smiles were identical. They both liked the same kind of music and downhill skiing. One way they were very different, however, was in how they handled difficulties. When Marc was upset, he would sit in his apartment stewing for hours. He often felt depressed. When something was bothering Kevin, he would share his feelings with someone, do what he could to fix it, and then try to let it go, knowing that dwelling on it would only make him feel worse. As a result, Kevin felt depressed far less often than Marc.

When the boys found out their parents were moving, they were both upset. They talked about it, agreeing that they wished their parents could stay in their current home. Then, Marc went home and started thinking about how his life would be changing. Marc continued to dwell on all the hard parts of his parents' upcoming move, and he finally fell asleep feeling depressed. The next morning, he didn't feel like getting up, much less going to work.

Kevin was also upset about the move. He thought about what a big change it would make in his life and how he would miss his parents. He even went to his best friend's house and told him about it. After talking about it a while, Kevin said, "Well, there's nothing I can do to change it, and we still have plans for the movies. Let's go." The friends went to see a great movie, and Kevin came home feeling good.

Whenever he found himself feeling sad or concerned about the move, he would talk with his friends about it and then turn his mind to something else.

Facing the same situation, Marc felt depressed because he held on to the negative thoughts. Kevin felt happier because he talked about these thoughts and then he let them go.

What to Do

Kevin was able to let go of his negative thoughts by talking with someone about them and then turning his mind to something else. There are other ways to help yourself let go as well.

On a separate sheet of paper, describe a problem that has been making you feel depressed lately. Write about it in as much detail as you can. Then, choose one of the methods below to physically let go of what you have written, and do it.

- Rip up your paper into tiny pieces and throw it into the garbage.

- Put your paper through a shredder.

- Read what you have written to someone else and then give that person the paper and ask him or her to rip it up in front of you.

- Burn your paper in a fireplace.

- Poke a long stick through your paper and burn it over a grill.

- Write your problem on bathroom tissue instead of regular paper and flush it down the toilet.

As you destroy your problem, tell yourself, *I am letting go of this. I will not let it depress me anymore.*

More to Do

Sit quietly and comfortably where you will not be disturbed. Close your eyes and picture yourself in vivid detail doing one of the following:

- You wrap your problem in a box and seal it very securely with strong tape and rope. Then you attach the box to a very powerful rocket. You take the rocket to an outdoor area where there are no houses, trees, or other obstructions. You light the rocket and stand back. You watch as the rocket blasts off into the sky with great speed and force. You watch it carry your problem quickly and powerfully away from you. You watch until it's completely out of sight, far off beyond the pull of Earth's gravity, continuing to travel farther into space. As you watch it go, you say to yourself, *I am letting go of this. I will not let it depress me anymore.*

- You wrap your problem in a box and seal it very securely with strong tape and rope. Then, you travel to a place far from where you live. You come to the edge of an ocean. If the climate is warm, you set the box onto a very fragile raft. If the climate is cold, you set the box onto a very fragile ice floe. You push the raft or the ice floe out into the sea, where the current catches it and carries it farther and farther away from you. You watch it until it's completely out of sight. As you watch it go, you say to yourself, *I am letting go of this. I will not let it depress me anymore.*

You may repeat either of these exercises as many times as you like, experimenting with different methods. If neither of these exercises was helpful to you the first time, try doing them using a different method from the list. Then, think up your own safe way to destroy your paper or another visualization that is effective for you.

14: HEALTHY SELF-ESTEEM

What to Know

People's self-esteem reflects the manner and degree to which they value themselves. People who have healthy self-esteem see themselves in a positive yet realistic way. People whose self-esteem is not healthy often have an overly negative view of themselves. When you have healthy self-esteem, you are less likely to feel depressed.

What to Do

Rate your self-esteem on the scale below, where 1 represents the worst you can possibly feel about yourself, and 10 represents the best you can possibly feel about yourself.

1 — 2 — 3 — 4 — 5 — 6 — 7 — 8 — 9 — 10

Then, on a separate sheet of paper, make a line down the middle. List your inner qualities that you feel are positive in the left column of the page; in the right column, list your inner qualities that you feel are negative. The qualities you list could include anything from the kind of friend you are, to whether you tend to be honest or deceptive, to whether you have a good sense of humor or are more of a sore loser.

Then, below these lists, list things that you are good at doing in the left column and things that you need to improve at doing in the right column. These could include anything from playing soccer to being punctual to cleaning your room or caring for your pet.

If you don't have as many items listed in your left (positive) columns as you do in your right (negative) columns, add more to the left column. If you can't think of enough by yourself, ask a friend or family member to help you. Don't stop until you have as many items listed in the left columns as in the right.

After looking at your lists, rate your self-esteem again.

1 — 2 — 3 — 4 — 5 — 6 — 7 — 8 — 9 — 10

More to Do

Reflect on why you gave yourself the rating you did on the first scale. How would you explain any difference between your first and second ratings?

How do you think you developed the self-esteem that you have now? From where or from whom did you learn to feel positive or negative about yourself?

How does your self-esteem affect whether you feel happy or depressed?

What changes could you make in your view of yourself that would help you have healthier self-esteem?

If you did end up asking other people, what did it feel like for you to ask other people about your strengths and weaknesses?

Some people think that focusing on their strengths makes them conceited. Being conceited means that you often brag about your strengths to others and you rarely admit to having faults. Healthy self-esteem involves being realistic, which means that you recognize, accept, and admit to both your strengths and your weaknesses.

15: FOLLOW MEANINGFUL PURSUITS

What to Know

Activity is a remedy for depression. The question is, what activities are right for you?

Life is so much more than trying to negate negatives, such as depression. The more time you spend in meaningful pursuits, the less time you'll spend absorbed in depressive thoughts, feelings, and behavioral habits.

In the process of curbing depression, it's never too early or too late to think about engaging in a positive or passionate pursuit. A passionate pursuit is more than a planned disruption of depression, such as watching a butterfly in flight. It may be studying butterflies and searching for them in their natural habitat over the course of a day or even a whole week.

Reengaging in a pursuit that you enjoyed in the past may reactivate your interest and help you feel less depressed.

What to Do

Positive activities can distract you from negative thoughts and bring about a change of mood. Make a list of brief activities you'd ordinarily like to do if you did not feel depressed. They may include soaking in a tub of warm water, putting up a bird feeder, or listening to a favorite song. Try to list as many as you can. Maybe it's something you do all the time, maybe it's something you only did once, but loved. Schedule and do a favorite activity each day.

Use this activity list you just generated to note former pleasures too. Then do the activity again, even if you don't feel like it. You can also make use of the serotonin-boosting properties of companionship by inviting a bummer buddy (see Activity 12) to join you.

16: IDENTIFY WHAT CAN'T BE CHANGED

What to Know

You've probably heard all or part of the Serenity Prayer— the poem that reads "give me the strength to accept the things I cannot change." There is a lot of wisdom in that phrase. But when we are depressed, we can sometimes lose track of things we can change, or the courage to accept things we can't.

Take a few minutes to study the aspects of Bill's situation, listed below, from the perspective of the Serenity Prayer. Does Bill know what he can and cannot control in his current situation? Is he practicing acceptance of the aspects that can't be controlled? Is he exerting control over the things that he can control? For items that Bill can't change, label them A for acceptance. For aspects he has control over, label them C for control.

Events or Situations in Bill's Life

1. Bill suffered an on-the-job injury.

2. Bill experiences back pain on a daily basis.

3. Bill was denied a disability pension.

4. Bill has thoughts that he has too much pain to work at any job.

5. Bill refuses to go through vocational retraining.

6. Bill underwent an unsuccessful back surgery that left him with more pain.

7. Bill spends a lot of time on his sofa to control the pain.

8. Bill doesn't go to church.

9. Bill doesn't exercise regularly because of the pain.

10. Bill takes larger and larger doses of narcotics to control his pain.

11. Bill experiences burning and stinging sensations in his back.

12. Bill experiences sensations of tingling and numbness in his leg.

13. Bill feels angry and irritable when in pain.

14. Bill remembers the injury.

15. Bill thinks about how he could have prevented the injury.

16. Bill yells at his children.

17. Bill is short with his wife.

18. Bill doesn't have sexual relations with his wife because his back hurts.

19. Bill has thoughts that life has given him a raw deal.

20. Bill has thoughts that he would be better off dead.

More to Do

As we assess Bill's situation, it becomes clear that Bill has some control over quite a few things. He can influence the amount of time he spends on the sofa, his attendance at church, his participation in daily exercises, his use of narcotics, his behavior toward his wife and children, and his sexual relationship with his wife. And he could choose to challenge his assumptions about his pain and try vocational retraining. Do these answers surprise you?

Now, take a closer look at the events and experiences that Bill has no immediate control over. In this category are not just the physical sensations Bill feels but also the spontaneous thoughts, feelings, and memories related to his pain and his personal history. Being in pain causes predictable private experiences, including negative emotions and thoughts. Unpleasant feelings, thoughts, and images show up in the moment for all of us in response to pain. They also show up even more when we try to suppress or avoid them. So, what we have to do instead is observe them, then decide what to do in response, according to our values.

The next time you find yourself in a depressive situation like Bill's, try to identify what you can change, and what you can't. And when it comes to the aspects of your situation or private experiences you can't change, look to what you can decide to do about these experiences. Depression is unpleasant and hard—but when you can respond to your situation with intention and agency, it makes it easier not to be so stuck.

17: SLEEP HYGIENE 101

What to Know

Studies show that knowledge about sleep hygiene improves sleep hygiene practices, which in turn improves sleep quality (Brown, Buboltz, and Soper 2002). So, just by reading this, you're on the right track. And here are some more concrete tips to prepare your brain for a great night's sleep.

What to Do

- **Sleep for eight hours straight.** Most people need about eight hours of sleep. In general, the older you are, the less sleep you need. In college, you need about eight hours and twenty-four minutes. By the time you start drawing Social Security, you might need only seven. The important thing is to sleep in one continuous block (seven hours plus a one-hour nap is not the same). So, don't take regular naps—and if you consistently get quality sleep in one solid block every night, you won't even feel that you need naps.

- **Use your bed or bedroom for sleeping.** Don't do work in bed or in your bedroom. Don't surf the Internet. Don't watch television. If you use your bedroom only for sleeping, your brain will associate your bed only with sleep, which will induce sleepiness, like Pavlovian conditioning. Of course, it's also okay to have sex there.

- **Create a routine for preparing for sleep.** Develop a nightly ritual to separate yourself from the rest of your hectic day.

Your prefrontal cortex, in particular, needs to wind down, so if you're doing everything at sixty miles per hour and then plopping into bed, you may have difficulty falling asleep or getting quality sleep. A bedtime ritual might involve brushing your teeth, washing your face, going to the bathroom, then reading for a few minutes. Or you could include having a cup of herbal tea, reading to your kids, or saying your prayers—any relaxing activity. Meditation can also be helpful. Sex, too, is okay, but probably can't be relied upon as part of your regular routine (if it can, props to you).

- **Avoid caffeine near bedtime**. Even if you can fall asleep while caffeinated, caffeine disrupts proper sleep architecture (NREM and REM sleep cycles) and reduces sleep quality. So, no black tea, green tea, coffee, or Red Bull within a few hours of sleep.

- **Eat and drink in moderation**. Don't eat a large meal less than three hours before bedtime. Indigestion can interfere with sleep, and acid reflux is more common once you're horizontal. However, a small snack of simple food is okay, even helpful if hunger is a distraction. Similarly, thirst can disrupt sleep, so have a couple sips of water before bed. But don't chug a whole glass, or your bladder will wake you up in the middle of the night.

- **Don't use alcohol as a regular sleep aid**. A beer or a glass of wine can help you fall asleep faster, but alcohol disrupts your sleep architecture, so your night's not as restful. On top of that, the more often you use alcohol to fall asleep, the less it works. Lastly, alcohol abuse can lead to the same types of reduced slow-wave sleep and increased REM sleep that are seen in depression.

- **Exercise**. Make physical activity a regular part of your life. Exercise improves sleep by synchronizing circadian rhythms, reducing stress, decreasing REM sleep, and inducing numerous neurochemical changes. Exercising too close to bedtime, however, may make it difficult to fall asleep, so try to do it a few hours before.

18: CONVERT NEGATIVITY INTO POSITIVE GOALS

What to Know

When you are thinking pessimistically, missions and goals may sound good for someone else. You may see yourself as too depressed to care or too listless to act. You may find yourself in a pool of negativity so deep that you don't know how to begin to shift from self-absorbing thinking to an objective, self-observant approach.

Feeling discouraged is an ideal opportunity for you to identify and address some of your self-defeating thoughts and beliefs and convert your negativity into something positive. One depressive thought tends to trigger another: *I am lost. No one appreciates me. I can't get through this. I can't stand how I feel. I am useless.*

Although such pessimistic thoughts sound bleak, you can convert them into positive counterdepression goals.

Depressive Pessimistic Thought	Positive Alternative Goal
I am lost.	Find a bearing.
No one appreciates me.	Find exceptions to this statement.
I'll never get over feeling depressed.	Question hopeless-thinking assumptions.
I can't stand how I feel.	Learn to tolerate what I don't like.
I'm useless.	Question uselessness assumptions.

What to Do

Use a piece of paper, your planner, or reminders you set up on your phone to translate your own negative thinking into positive goals. Record some of your pessimistic thoughts. Then, convert them into positive statements of what you can do to change these thoughts.

19: YOU ARE FLAW-SOME

What to Know

This exercise requires you to practice self-compassion for your personal flaws, both real and imagined. There are two basic types of flaws that figure prominently in the negative self-stories we tend to beat ourselves up about. The first is some attribute we have that we find unacceptable, be it a receding hairline, the way we might stutter under stress, or our sense we're not as interesting as other people. The second type of flaw is something we believe we lack, like good looks, confidence in social situations, or public speaking ability.

What to Do

Take a few minutes now to identify the flaws you most dislike about yourself in both areas. Try to clearly describe the flaw and what you don't like about it.

Now that you have identified your flaws, it's time to practice being flaw-some! Read each of your flaws out loud, and at the end of each statement add in "and I love this part of me too!" As you recite this statement, put yourself into it, as much as you can. Try to create a mental space in which you relax, let go of attachment to self-rejection, and truly love even what you dislike about yourself.

Were you able to genuinely extend loving energy toward those things you dislike about yourself? If your mind is reactive, telling you that your flaw can't be accepted, practice acknowledging what your reactive mind has to say, detaching from it, and gently and purposefully redirecting your attention to loving yourself (see Activity 9). You could even take what your reactive mind told you and write that down as a flaw and make that part of your flaw-someness! The fact that you have a reactive mind that is unwilling to stop judging you is also a part of your flaw-someness. How cool is that?

20: AVOID AVOIDANCE

What to Know

Checking out at the supermarket, you're presented with an array of enticing candy bars and magazines. Do you stick to your shopping list or reach for a candy bar? The key to understanding impulses is that everything pleasurable releases dopamine in a specific part of your brain called the nucleus accumbens. Sex releases dopamine. Winning money releases dopamine. Drugs release dopamine. Chocolate releases dopamine.

The really interesting thing about the brain, however, is that it learns what's pleasurable and how to anticipate getting it. For example, when you eat a candy bar for the first time, dopamine is released. The next time you pick up a candy bar, dopamine is released as soon as you open the wrapper. And the next time, dopamine is released simply when you see the candy bar from across the room. Pretty soon, dopamine is released as soon as you walk into the store, just from the anticipation of seeing it, opening it, and eating it.

With impulses, something you do or sense triggers the anticipation of a specific pleasurable outcome. The problem is that the dopamine that is released in anticipation of pleasure actually motivates the actions that lead to that pleasure. Each step along the way gives you a little boost of dopamine that propels you on to the next step.

If you were a caveman, your impulses wouldn't be such a problem. Life would be pretty simple. If something tasted good, you'd eat as much as possible, and if something felt good, you'd do it as much as possible. Nowadays, though, there are too many easily obtainable pleasures, which hijack your brain with dopamine and create a tendency to act for immediate gratification.

It becomes even more problematic in depression, because when you're depressed, there's less dopamine activity in your brain in general. First, that means things that used to be enjoyable no longer are. Second, with reduced dopamine activity, the only things that motivate are things that release lots of dopamine, such as junk food, drugs, gambling, and porn. All these impulses mean your actions are guided only by what's most immediately pleasurable, which is not usually good for you in the long term. And while most impulses are easy to recognize, bad habits—which insidiously become routine— are more difficult to spot.

What to Do

1. Figure out your triggers. It's much easier to avoid temptation than to resist it. If you know what triggers a particular habit, sometimes you can get rid of that habit simply by removing that trigger from your life. For example, Billie realized he was watching too much television, and the trigger was seeing the television set itself. He moved it out of his bedroom, and now, he doesn't have a problem watching too much television. As another example, if you don't want to buy cookies, don't walk down the cookie aisle at the supermarket. Seeing all those delicious baked goods will release dopamine and push you toward buying them.

2. Take a deep breath. When you start to feel antsy or compelled to act on a bad habit, take a deep breath. Let it out slowly, then take another deep breath. Repeat as necessary. Long, slow breathing calms the brain's stress response.

3. Look back at the activity list that you made earlier in the book, if you did Activity 3—or make your own list of activities you find pleasurable now. Whenever you feel triggered toward doing something you know is a bad habit, like binge-watching TV or overeating, go to your activities list instead.

21: THE FREE TRIAL MEMBERSHIP

What to Know

Just as exercise strengthens your muscles, it also strengthens your brain. Numerous studies have demonstrated that exercise causes growth of new neurons. In one study, a pair of Texas scientists looked at the effects of exercise on rats (Leasure and Jones 2008). The rats were divided into three groups: voluntary running, forced running, and controls. Those in the voluntary running group were allowed to run at whatever speed they felt like, while those in the forced group had to run at a set speed. The controls weren't allowed to run at all.

The study showed that both exercise groups had greater development of new neurons in the hippocampus—the area of the brain that is in charge of learning and memory. However, the voluntary group had more new neurons than the forced group, which suggests that actively choosing to exercise provides more benefits than being forced to. It also suggests that while hitting the treadmill at the gym might not be as great as running through the park, it's much better than doing nothing. And in the end, all you need is something, no matter how small, that's better than what you're doing right now.

What to Do

Commit to a brief trial period. Sign up for an exercise class and commit to going to the first three. Check online sites like Groupon or LivingSocial for a monthlong trial to your local yoga or pilates studio at a discounted rate. Join a gym and promise yourself that, for the first two weeks, you'll go every Monday, Wednesday, and Friday. Even if you're feeling too tired to do any actual exercise, still go to the gym, park your car, walk in, change into workout clothes, and pick up one five-pound weight. If you're really so tired that you don't want to do anything else there, that's totally fine. You've fulfilled your obligation to yourself, and you can go home and rest until next time.

22: HUGS AND HANDSHAKES

What to Know

There are many ways to increase oxytocin (a hormone associated with feelings of love, trust, and empathy) or, generally, to activate brain circuits involved in being social. These often involve various forms of touching, like hugs and handshakes and massage. Talking with people—and sometimes just being around other people—also activates the social brain and can release oxytocin. Even pets can help release oxytocin.

What to Do

One of the primary ways to release oxytocin is through touching. Obviously, it's not always appropriate to touch most people, but small touches like handshakes and pats on the back are usually okay. For people you're close with, make more of an effort to touch them more often. Hugs, especially long ones, are particularly good at releasing oxytocin, as are orgasms.

You don't have to limit yourself to physical contact though; you could also turn up the heat. Feeling warm can boost oxytocin—or at least mimic its effects, increasing feelings of trust and generosity. So, if you can't get a hug, try wrapping yourself in a blanket and holding a mug of hot tea. Taking a warm shower can also help.

Massage reduces pain because the oxytocin system activates pain-killing endorphins. Massage also improves sleep and reduces fatigue by increasing serotonin and dopamine and decreasing the stress hormone cortisol. So, if you're feeling out of sorts, get a massage. You'll be actively triggering the neurotransmitter systems that work to make you happier.

PART 3

BEAT HOPELESSNESS AND LOW MOTIVATION

23: PROCRASTINATION FLIP TECHNIQUE

What to Know

If you find yourself thinking something like *I don't have the energy to change* or *I can't succeed, so why try?* you're boxed into a procrastination-depression way of thinking. To break this procrastination-depression connection, look for weak points in the connection. For example, if you have the energy to think depressing thoughts, you have the energy to think proactive thoughts, such as *I can slowly work my way up from under this malaise.*

By getting specific with yourself, you can change your perspective. You can convert your defeatist thought into an action-minded goal: *I will write a check to pay my mortgage at 2:00 p.m.* This action is definable, purposeful, measurable, and achievable. You also have a timeline that you can meet. By taking small, defined steps, you can stop procrastination thinking from obstructing your goals.

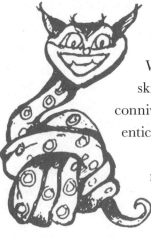

It helps to put a face on your inner procrastination voice. Let's give it the face of a Wheedler. Historically, this is a crafty creature skilled in subterfuge, beguilement, finagling, and conniving. I see the Wheedler as having a smiling, enticing, Cheshire cat's face.

And just as the Cheshire cat confused and manipulated Alice, your inner Wheedler is trying to trick you into believing defeatist thoughts.

What to Do

The procrastination flip technique is a device for reversing a form of primitive reasoning that, left unchecked, fuels procrastination. The flip technique is to do the opposite of what your Wheedler tells you. Here is an example of how to use the flip technique.

Wheedler Thinking: *Take a break before you start your antidepression program. Read the newspaper. Play solitaire. Get out that pool cue and start a game.*

Flip Your Thinking: *Work at your antidepression goal for an hour and take a ten-minute break by reading your favorite newspaper column. After the next hour of chipping away at your project, play ten minutes of solitaire. After the next hour, play a game of pool.*

Wheedler Thinking: *Don't think about going to the gym. Wait. You'll feel rested and ready. Perhaps you'll go in a day or so. Besides, exercise as a remedy for depression won't work if you're depressed.*

Flip Your Thinking: *Put one foot in front of the other and head to the gym.*

Wheedler Thinking: *Get into a squabble with your mate. That will stimulate you more than setting antidepression priorities and goals.*

Flip Your Thinking: *Get started on setting goals and making plans. Get in front of the computer, boot up, and type the letters of the alphabet to break the inertia of inaction. Then, continue with setting a meaningful, measurable, and attainable antidepression goal.*

Wheedler Thinking: *Activity remedies for depression, like cleaning, are a pain and waste of time. You have better things to do, like watching your favorite soap opera.*

Flip Your Thinking: *Start cleaning the house while listening to the soap opera. Here, you are doing two things at once: one active and one passive.*

Now, you try. Identify your procrastination-depression thought and flip it.

24: THE "JUST DO IT" METHOD

What to Know

When you procrastinate, it's like riding a horse that is taking you somewhere you don't want to go. The horse is like the powerful primitive brain, which goes for pleasure and avoids pain. When the horse is in control, it goes where it wants, and its inclination is to follow its usual pathways to familiar places. The rider, on the other hand, is the rational side of your personality that overrides impulse. Instead of automatically collapsing in despair, your rider guides the corrective actions that you take.

What happens when you become the rider—when you take the reins and direct the horse that is your brain toward antidepression actions? Again, you're likely to experience conflict. At first, you may experience strong resistance. The horse won't budge. But you grip the reins. You channel the horse's energy and strength into a new direction. This takes mental effort, but by using your higher mental powers productively, you are less likely to be diverted.

What to Do

Florida psychologist Robert Heller once suggested a way to block the downward spiral of depression. He noted that when they're depressed, people tend to withdraw from others and from many activities of daily living, and they spiral downward with an increasing sense of isolation and loneliness. The key to changing this dynamic is to interrupt the pattern. As an alternative, Heller suggests a "just do it" technique where you initially act without inspiration. And he takes the position that by changing your behavior, you can shift your focus from depressive thoughts and premonitions to antidepression actions.

To make use of this insight, keep an activity log as a motivational tool. The purpose of the log is to keep track of what you do each day and to gradually and consistently add activities, regardless of how you feel. This record also provides a way to measure your progress over time. It could be a journal by your bed where you input all the things you did that day. Or a small notebook you take with you and note what you do as it's happening. You could even get creative and post Instagram live stories that you can rewatch later.

The other key to this exercise is to set aside time to review what you've been doing. Through reviewing your ongoing record, you can recognize gaps in your activities, say, where you avoid personal contacts that might help curb loneliness. You might then add activities where you spend time with others. This can include such simple gestures as greeting your neighbors or asking a store clerk where a product may be found. Instead of shopping once a week, you might choose to shop for a different basic item each day.

To benefit from this method, continue doing this exercise even if you experience no initial pleasure. After all, a prime feature of depression is a loss of pleasure. This exercise paves a path to feeling better.

25: CHALLENGE HOPELESSNESS

What to Know

You can be in a hopeless position when you're stuck in rush-hour traffic on the way to the airport with only twenty minutes before your flight takes off. Hopelessness in depression is another matter. Here, you have options to act in some way, even if the actions are small— and yet you often believe you just can't change. In this mindset, you have no possibility of succeeding, improving, getting help, or finding a solution.

But this idea of hopelessness is a myth. Like the Sirens, who captivated the minds of sailors and lured them to shipwreck and disaster, such fatalistic thoughts can transfix you.

Hopelessness is a myth because the human mind is made for adaptability. We can generate different ideas, make predictions, and move toward positive future opportunities. We can avoid excessive risks and visible dangers. We can solve problems. Yet, we sometimes forget that these capabilities are within reach—if we reach for them. This activity focuses on an adaptive approach to deal with your sense of hopelessness.

What to Do

The key to this approach is to take time to dispute your hopeless thoughts. Ask your hopeless mind a question as a starting point, then answer the question by exploring the options you have at hand. See below for examples.

Hopeless thought: *I don't have what it takes to change.*

Ask it a question: *What can I work at changing that is both worthwhile and within my control to do?*

Answer the question: *I started exercising to work against depressive sensations and mood. I've made progress. I can make positive changes, and I'm doing that already.*

Hopeless thought: *I'm going to suffer forever.*

Ask it a question: *Where is the proof that my mood will remain constantly negative?*

Answer the question: *The answer is that there is no proof that my depressed mood will continue forever. Education about depression gives me a different prediction. The odds favor that I will learn to manage symptoms of depression. Unrealistic ideas are subject to evaluation and revision. Physical exercise helps boost endorphins, or feel-good brain chemicals. In short, I have many ways to change that I have the power to initiate.*

Hopelessness can be among the more painful of the depressive themes. But the belief that change is impossible is not provable. If you like, you can write down the options you have. It might be good to place them in places you see a lot, or enter them as reminders in your phone—that way you'll be surrounded by ideas of how to move forward through hopelessness.

26: STRANDED

What to Know

This exercise will help get you in the mood to do some serious work on clarifying your values. We recommend downloading the audio version of this exercise at http://www.newharbinger.com/50065; the guided audio component will make this exercise an enjoyable and powerful experience for you. Allow yourself about ten minutes of uninterrupted time to complete this exercise. Close your eyes to help you better imagine the scenario. Just relax, go along with the prompts, and be open to where it takes you. The more you put into it, the more you'll get out of it.

What to Do

Imagine that you're on a trip to the South Pacific, and during a sight-seeing trip in a small boat you rented, you experience engine trouble. As your boat starts to drift toward the breakers, you realize that you'll have to swim to a nearby island to avoid a catastrophe. You swim for your life, and you end up on the shore of a tiny deserted island. You sleep in the sun, and when you are rested, you awaken and take stock of your surroundings. You look around and find some interesting things to eat and a protected place where you can rest. You realize that you have no way to communicate where you are, as everything was left in the rental boat. You hope that eventually you'll be found, but you don't know when that might happen.

Then, your thoughts turn to your family and friends—the people back home. They will hear that you've disappeared without a trace and are presumed dead at sea. There will be tears. They will come together and speak of you and your life. They don't know that you're okay and that you'll be back with them soon. Eventually, they decide to remember you in a memorial service. They agree to write eulogies and come together to share them with each other to remember you. Eulogies usually speak to the more lasting qualities a person is remembered for and the impact they had on the lives of those they left behind.

Imagine now that you can be there unobserved, like an invisible bird flying above them, and you listen to these heartfelt speeches of acknowledgment. What does your life partner say about you as a person? How does your life partner describe you as a lover, a companion, and a playmate? If you have a child or children, what words do they use to describe your life and your advice about living life? How do they sum up your efforts to prepare them to go forward without you? What would your friends, your coworkers, and your neighbors say? What would people say about your spiritual life? What would you hear about your participation in the community in which you live? How do the mourners remember you in terms of your ability to have fun, relax, or engage in leisure activities?

More to Do

Once you have completed this imaginary exercise, take a few minutes to reflect on these questions, or write your answers down in a journal or on your phone.

Based on how I'm living my life right now, what did I hear in the eulogy...

...from my partner?

...from my children?

...from my closest friends?

...from my coworkers?

...from members of my community?

...from people in my spiritual community?

If I could have lived my life any way I wanted to, what would I like to have heard...

...from my partner?

...from my children?

...from my closest friends?

...from my coworkers?

...from members of my community?

...from members of my spiritual community?

Is there a difference between what you think you'd hear if the memorial service were held today and what you'd ideally like to hear? Any differences give you important information. First, look at what you wrote down for what you would most likely hear based on how you're living right now. You probably listed some things that warmed your heart, since you certainly do things that reflect your values that are noticed by loved ones. At the same time, you may have written down things you're not very proud of. This is something to pay attention to, because it might be an invitation for you to do some corrective work in that area. By the way, we all have those areas, so don't get down on yourself about it!

Second, comparing what you would currently hear with what you'd ideally like to hear at your memorial service highlights values that you may have placed on the back burner. These may be important values that are being undermined by your avoidance of emotionally charged life problems or that just have not been prioritized recently. What steps can you take to bring your life as is now more in line with your life as you'd like it to be?

27: OBSERVE YOUR JUDGMENTS

What to Know

This exercise will help you practice distinguishing between describing things and judging things.

In this exercise, you'll study an object in your environment, a person you know, and an event in your past. For each, we ask that you observe your reactive mind's tendency to be more interested in judgments than facts. When you notice this happening—for example, if you end up judging the chair you're sitting on for being too stiff to be comfortable—just say to yourself, *Thank you, mind, for giving me the evaluation that...*, for example, *Thank you, mind, for giving me the evaluation that this chair is too stiff to be comfortable.* This exercise also gives you an opportunity to see similarities and differences between your reactive mind's responses to objects, people, and events.

What to Do

Select an object that you want to focus your concentration on for few minutes: a teacup, a piece of furniture, a picture, a flower arrangement, anything specific. Concentrate on this object for a few minutes, focusing only on describing—not judging—the object. Write out your description of the object on any piece of paper you have on hand.

Next, write down any judgments that may have crept in.

Finally, thank your reactive mind for handing you each of these judgments.

Now, do the same for a person—describe this person, using only descriptions, not judgments.

What judgments are creeping in? Remember that with people, judgments may involve the person's state of mind, what you think the person thinks of you, or what you think is good or bad about that person. Write the judgments down.

Finally, thank your reactive mind for handing you each of these judgments.

Now, bring to mind a difficult event in your life. It could be from your childhood, teenage, or adult years. Choose something that's been a problem for you in terms of the emotional reactions it triggers. Focus your mind's eye on this event until you're sure you have the image in full detail; then, write your description of the actual event.

Note any judgments that creep in as you write. These may include how the event affects you now, how it has changed your life, or evaluations of right and wrong or good and bad, such as "What I did was disgusting" or "What she said was thoughtless." Write the judgments down.

Once again, thank your reactive mind for handing you these judgments.

More to Do

What did you notice as you proceeded through this exercise? Often, our reactive mind tends to insert more evaluations as the emotional stakes become higher. Setting aside your judgments about a cup is very different than setting aside your judgments about a painful personal memory. You might have noticed that you remembered your painful life event primarily in terms of judgments about it. For some people, judgments are so built in that it's actually hard to get back to the original event and describe it in factual, objective terms. Practicing this technique will help you identify your judgments so you can let go of them.

28: LOVING-KINDNESS PRACTICE

What to Know

There are a variety of meditation practices associated with the development of compassion, and these are sometimes referred to as loving-kindness meditation practices. We recommend that you start with a brief daily practice.

What to Do

Your first practice efforts will be using key compassion phrases directed toward a benefactor, or someone who showed a strong interest in you and went out of their way to help you learn and grow— someone who was gentle with you when you made mistakes and curious and encouraging about your potential as a human being. Not everyone can identify a benefactor, so if no one comes to mind right away, you might select a friend instead. It's best to choose someone who is generous and loving toward you, and someone with whom you do not have a sexual relationship. It's also best to choose someone who is alive—but it's okay to choose someone who has passed on as well. Spend a few days or up to a few weeks practicing the following wishes for this chosen person:

May you be safe.

May you be healthy.

May you be happy.

May you have ease of being.

May you know peace.

Next, begin directing statements toward strangers. You might try the first person you see on a morning walk. Do this for several days.

May you be safe.

May you be healthy.

May you be happy.

May you have ease of being.

May you know peace.

Finally, direct compassion statements toward yourself:

May you be safe.

May you be healthy.

May you be happy.

May you have ease of being.

May you know peace.

Whoever is the focus of your compassion (benefactor, friend, stranger, or self), always try to include a sequence in which you direct your wishes for compassion to a larger group (the people on your block, the people in your city, all beings in this world). For most people, it's easier to be compassionate toward others, so this approach helps you take advantage of that.

Practice daily at whatever time is convenient and for five to thirty minutes, focusing on the wishes and the target of those wishes. Concentrate your efforts on creating images, emotions, and sensations consistent with your wishes. And feel free to use your own words to express your love and kindness! See what effect loving-kindness might have on your mood and your ability to be kind to others and to yourself.

29: MAKE SNAP DECISIONS

What to Know

One thing that makes humans special is the fact that we have such a large prefrontal cortex. The prefrontal cortex allows us to solve complex math problems, assemble Ikea furniture, send astronauts to the moon, and throw successful dinner parties.

Think of a chess game. How do you know which move to make? You look at the board and run through a mental simulation. You could move your knight, but then your opponent could take your bishop, although it would expose his or her king. So, you should move your bishop first, then your opponent can't take it after you move your knight. All of those thoughts happen in the prefrontal cortex. It's like a virtual reality machine that allows you to imagine the future and predict the consequences of your actions.

What's the difference between planning and worrying? The answer is really just the amount of emotional and self-oriented processing—how vigorously your prefrontal cortex reacts to potential future scenarios. Planning and problem solving both involve projecting yourself or other pieces of information into the future and evaluating how you would feel about a particular outcome. Worrying has that same feature but is colored with more negative emotions. Worrying worsens your mood, and when your mood is worse, you worry more, which is a classic downward spiral.

What to Do

Make a decision. Anxiety and worrying are provoked by possibility, not certainty. In fact, many people are less happy when they have more choices because they have more to worry about. When everything is up in the air, the amygdala becomes more reactive. The amygdala is the part of the brain that modulates emotional responses—it guards your brain against threats and, in contrast to the prefrontal cortex, reacts instantly when they arise. So, if you tend to worry, reduce your options and make quick decisions whenever possible. As soon as you make a decision, however small, everything starts to feel more manageable.

30: THE ANTI-LAZINESS RULE

What to Know

One of the greatest obstacles to exercise is that people with depression don't feel like doing it. Thinking about exercise is often accompanied by automatic negative thoughts like, *Oh, that's not gonna help.* But that's just because the depressed brain is stuck in a depressed loop and doesn't know how to get out.

There is no one solution to the problem of motivation. But this also means that any little thing you can do is a step in the right direction. Every minute you walk instead of sitting on the couch is a jump-start to an upward spiral of feeling better.

Remember that even if it doesn't feel like the exercise is working, it's still causing tons of unnoticed brain changes. It's modifying circuits, releasing positive neurochemicals, and reducing stress hormones. So, stop worrying about whether each step will make you feel better. Stop asking, *Am I feeling better yet?* Just absorb yourself in the task of living your life.

What to Do

Make anti-laziness your rule. For instance, decide ahead of time that you'll take the stairs for anything less than three floors. Decide that you'll walk to do any errand that is less than a mile away or bike to any destinations that are less than two miles away. Commit to never taking an escalator if the stairs are right next to it. Don't circle the parking lot looking for a closer space, just take the first one you see. See if this practice helps start you on the spiral to still other new behaviors.

31: GIVE YOURSELF AFFIRMATIONS

What to Know

Two studies from the United Kingdom figured out a clever way to help change your bad habits (Armitage, Harris, Hepton, and Napper 2008; Epton and Harris 2008). The trick is self-affirmation, which may sound hokey, but the results were undeniable. The first study had smokers answer a set of questions. Members of the control group were asked somewhat random questions about their opinions, such as "Is chocolate the best flavor of ice cream?" But those in the "self-affirmation" group were asked questions that made them focus on the best parts of themselves: "Have you ever forgiven another person when they have hurt you?" or "Have you ever been considerate of another person's feelings?" If the participants answered yes, they were asked to elaborate, which served to draw their attention to their positive qualities. Then, both groups read an informational packet on the negative health effects of smoking.

The study found that smokers in the self-affirmation group developed a greater intention to quit smoking and also were more likely to start looking into how to quit. Importantly, the effect of self-affirmation was strongest on the heaviest smokers. This means that for the people who are the worst off, a little self-affirmation does the most good.

Studies show that thinking about your positive qualities makes it easier to change your habits. That's a cool phenomenon.

What to Do

Answer this list of questions with a yes or a no. If you answer yes to any questions, please elaborate the details. Get as specific about the situations, and your virtues, as you can:

- Have you ever forgiven another person when he or she has hurt you?

- Have you ever been considerate of another person's feelings?

- Have you ever given money or items to someone less fortunate than you?

- Have you ever tried to cheer up someone who had had a bad day?

- Have you ever encouraged a friend to pursue a goal?

Now, look back at what you've written. Does seeing the positive things you've done make it easier for you to summon the resolve to do something that you find difficult or change a habit you'd rather not indulge? Consider which affirmations you can take with you into your day-to-day life, especially on days you're struggling.

32: WRITE A THANK-YOU LETTER

What to Know

When you feel depressed, life is full of disappointments and lacking in things you sorely need—a good night's sleep, a job well done, a friendly face. But while the gap between what you want and what you have may seem large, it's never as wide as it appears when you're weighed down by depression. What's more, there's a powerful force that directly combats negativity, and it's called "gratitude."

Gratitude is a potent antidote to negativity because it doesn't depend on your life circumstances. You could be poor and starving and yet still grateful for a warm breeze. Conversely, you could be rich and powerful and still be annoyed at the sound your husband makes when he's chewing—or devastated when you lose someone close to you. Gratitude is a state of mind—in fact, there's a gratitude circuit in your brain, badly in need of a workout. Strengthening that circuit brings you the power to elevate your physical and mental health, boost happiness, improve sleep, and help you feel more connected to other people. Importantly, the effect of gratitude is greatest in people with the highest levels of hopelessness. When everything appears bleak and meaningless, a little gratitude goes a long way.

Gratitude also reduces anxiety. Both worry and anxiety arise out of the possibility that something bad might happen. But the brain can only focus on so many things at once, so when you're thankful for the good things that might occur in the future, gratitude replaces those negative feelings, and the worry evaporates.

What to Do

Think of someone who has been especially kind to you—a friend, a teacher, a coworker—whom you've never properly thanked. Write a letter thanking this person, being specific about what he or she did that affected your life. Then, schedule a meeting, maybe over coffee or a drink, and deliver the letter in person. Don't tell the person what the meeting is about; let it be a surprise. This form of gratitude can have a long-lasting effect. One study showed that after writing and delivering a thank-you letter, people had increased levels of happiness even two months later (Froh, Yurkewicz, and Kashdan 2009).

PART 4

MAKE EASY HABIT CHANGES THAT YOU'LL THANK YOURSELF FOR LATER

33: FOOD TO HELP YOUR MOOD

What to Know

When the chemicals in our brains that regulate mood become imbalanced, depression can be triggered or heightened. Because the food that we put into our bodies affects the chemicals in our brains, eating particular foods can alter our moods.

A good diet is just one aspect of self-care, and it won't fix everything—but paying attention to your diet and practicing healthy nutrition may help you relieve, and even prevent, feelings of depression.

While each person's chemical make-up is a little different, there are some vitamins and nutrients that have been shown to affect brain chemicals in many people. These include the B-complex vitamins (folic acid in particular), omega-3 fatty acids, sugar, caffeine, and alcohol.

Vitamin B-12 is found in meat, dairy products, and eggs. All the other B vitamins are found mainly in whole grain products and fortified cereals, meats, leafy green vegetables, nuts, and seeds. Folic acid (vitamin B-9) is also found in citrus fruits, strawberries and cantaloupe, asparagus, liver, beans, and legumes (dried beans and peas). When your body is low in folic acid and other B vitamins, you may have more feelings of depression.

Omega-3 fatty acids are found in cold-water fish, such as tuna and salmon. These fatty acids have been found to play a crucial role in the function of brain chemicals. If your body is low in these acids, you may have stronger feelings of depression.

White sugar is found in candy, cookies, cakes, ice cream, soda, and many cereals. Caffeine is found in cola drinks, other sodas, tea, and coffee. Both these substances have been linked to higher levels of depression. While sugar and caffeine may give you an initial energy boost, the body's blood sugar then drops very quickly, and sluggishness and fatigue can set in.

Finally, alcohol is often used as an escape from depression, but since it affects the body by depressing the central nervous system, it actually makes depression worse. Alcohol can also lead to vitamin deficiencies that can contribute to higher levels of depression.

Along with the information about particular foods that affect our brain chemicals, it's also important to know that a healthy diet is, in general, better for avoiding depression than one that is unhealthy. Typically, a healthy diet includes more fresh, natural foods and fewer processed or packaged foods. It has a balance of fruits and vegetables, grains, proteins, and dairy products. It also includes a variety of foods from each of those categories. When you are eating a healthy diet, your body and mind function better, and you are better able to handle the ups and downs of daily life. When you are eating an unhealthy diet, you have less physical and emotional energy to ward off feelings of depression.

What to Do

Keep track of your food and beverage intake and your level of depressive feelings for one week. Record everything you eat or drink, and record your depression level three times each day. Rate your depression from 1 to 5, with 1 being very low and 5 being very high.

More to Do

Look back at the information you have recorded about yourself. Do you see any patterns in your depression level? For example, do you seem to feel more depressed in the morning, afternoon, or evening?

Compare the amount you eat of foods that may increase depression (sugar, caffeine, alcohol) to the amount you eat of foods that may decrease depression (those with B vitamins or omega-3 fatty acids). Describe what you notice:

- As you review your food consumption, determine if your diet is more healthy or unhealthy.

- Describe how you do or do not eat a variety of foods and a balance of foods from different groups.

- Describe how you do or do not eat fresh and unprocessed foods.

- Describe any connection you notice between what you put into your body and your level of depression.

- Reflect on how you could realistically improve your diet to improve your mood.

When you begin to implement a successful diet change, see what effect it has on your mood and your ability to deal with the tough things you might face. Do you find you have more energy and a greater degree of calm and flexibility?

34: ACT ON THE A'S

What to Know

Most people feel stress almost on a daily basis. When you do not know how to manage stress, it's easy to feel depressed, because you often feel anxious, tired, or overwhelmed. Learning stress-management techniques can help you ward off feelings of depression. Here are three simple ones you can try.

1. Avoid it. Remove yourself from stressful situations when you can; do not purposely put yourself into situations that you know are highly stressful for you; do not dwell on thoughts that raise your stress level.

2. Adjust. If there's no way to avoid a stressful situation, or you find yourself in one anyway, do what you can to change the situation so it's less stressful.

3. Alter your thinking. If you can't change something, change your thoughts about it so you don't perceive it as so stressful. Or change the way you cope with it so you can handle it better.

For example, Anna loved art, but it also caused her stress. Her private lessons took up a lot of time in her already busy schedule; and she often compared herself to others in the group class and felt she was not a very good artist.

So, Anna tried to act on the A's. She thought about avoiding art altogether, but she knew she didn't want to do that because she enjoyed it so much. She thought about making adjustments and realized she could cut back on her painting lessons or drop another hobby to give herself more time. She also decided that art was more important to her than some of the other hobbies in her schedule, so she dropped archery.

Then, she thought about how she could alter her thinking. She decided to stop comparing herself to others in her class; it didn't help her and only made her feel stressed. She also decided to stop worrying about the future. If she didn't make professional art, she could still paint as a hobby and enjoy it just as much.

The changes Anna made to the way she engaged with art gave her a lot more time to practice it. She also didn't feel as pressured and she found herself enjoying her painting time more than before. Her stress level went down, and her feelings of depression subsided.

What to Do

Make a list of the situations in your own life that feel stressful to you. Put them in order from most to least stressful.

Then, for each situation, write how you can act on the A's to help yourself manage the stress. Is there anything stress-inducing in the situations that you can Avoid? Are there any aspects of the situations you can Adjust? Are there ways you can Alter your thinking about these situations to make them less stressful and overwhelming?

35: GET OUTSIDE YOURSELF

What to Know

Feelings of depression tend to grow when people dwell on their own problems. Focusing away from yourself, or getting "outside" yourself, can help you feel better. One effective way to do this is to focus on helping someone else who is in need.

Chantelle felt depressed because she was lonely. Even in a crowd of people, she often felt as if she had no friends. She just didn't feel connected to anyone. When she joined the Volunteer Committee at her office, Chantelle was asked to help at different places in the community that needed extra support. One week, she read stories to children who were in the cancer unit of the hospital. The next week, she and the other club members sang holiday songs at the senior citizens' home. The week after that, Chantelle collected canned goods and clothing for people whose homes had been destroyed by a hurricane.

Each time Chantelle came home from a volunteer event, she found herself feeling less lonely inside. She realized that during the time she had been helping other people, she had stopped thinking about her own feelings of depression. She also realized that many people were in worse situations than she was, and she felt good because she could do something to help them. Finally, she found that she liked interacting with the people she helped. They were always so glad to see her.

What to Do

Think of someone you know who is hurting in some way, needs help with something, or needs cheering up. It might be a friend, family member, neighbor, school staff person, or anyone you know. Think of an act of kindness you could do for that person in the week ahead. Could you help with a chore? Send a card or an encouraging note? Buy that person a soda or cup of coffee? Listen to him or her? Write your ideas down somewhere.

Plan to carry out your idea. Tell when and how you will do this.

After you have carried out your plan, describe what happened.

How often did you think about your own feelings of depression while you were planning and carrying out this act of kindness?

How did you feel after you gave this gift of yourself?

More to Do

The activities listed below provide a number of opportunities for getting outside yourself and helping other people. Circle any that sound interesting to you:

tutoring children

reading to the blind

collecting recyclables

doing office work

delivering library books

raising money

painting houses

planning events

building houses

caring for animals

being a tour guide

being a camp counselor

giving blood

babysitting

visiting seniors

making phone calls

cleaning houses

having a bake sale

assisting teachers

doing walk-a-thons

coaching sports

translating

stuffing envelopes

playing in a band

delivering meals to homebound people

teaching English to foreign language speakers

preparing first-aid kits

cooking meals

writing to people in prison

mowing lawns

writing to soldiers

working with the disabled

serving food

answering a crisis hotline

visiting people in hospitals

making lunches for the homeless

You can also jot down any other volunteer activities that you would like to try on a separate piece of paper or in your phone.

Now, circle any of the skills or talents in the list below that you could teach to others:

sewing	woodworking
cooking	doing math
painting	interior decorating
playing cards	playing basketball
riding a bike	working on cars
gardening	drawing
keyboarding	singing
knitting	taking photographs
baking	using a computer
dancing	skateboarding
whistling	playing tennis
reading	scrapbooking
making jewelry	playing an instrument
playing chess	writing poetry
writing	caring for pets
swimming	boating
crafts	

List other skills or talents you have that aren't listed here on that same piece of paper or on your phone.

Now, choose one of the ideas you identified and imagine what you think it would be like for you to try helping someone with this activity.

You can find people who need help every day if you just look around. If you would like to try more organized volunteer work but don't know where to find it, start by calling your local hospital, place of worship, or village hall. You can also look on the Internet at http://www.networkforgood.org and http://www.volunteermatch.org.

36: OVERCOME DISCOMFORT DODGING

What to Know

Discomfort dodging is a common excuse for putting off activities that are good for you and aren't always the most fun to do, like exercising. This is where you default to easier or safer activities. Let's say that you like the benefits of exercising. You have good reason to believe that exercising can eventually bring you some relief from depression. At the same time, you are stewing about how bad you feel in a way that makes it hard for you to get out to get any exercise. Stewing is a diversion.

You come to a crossroads where you can choose between doing and stewing. Now, you face the timeless procrastination double-agenda dilemma. You want the benefits from exercising. You also want to avoid the discomfort of gearing up for exercise and exercising, especially when you already believe that you lack energy. That's the dilemma.

As you face the dilemma, you may experience a struggle of the mind against itself. Exercising takes effort and can be uncomfortable, so you get signals from your lower brain—the regions of the brain (like the amygdala) that are older than your prefrontal cortex and more focused on instinct and avoiding pain—not to do it. But you also know the long-term benefits of exercise, so your voice of reason says to do it. And you now have an opportunity to compromise with yourself. You can accept that exercising is uncomfortable and give your primitive brain its due. Then follow instructions from your enlightened reason.

What to Do

Here are additional ways to tip the balance in favor of a reasoned approach to exercising:

- Exercise even when you don't feel like it.

- Accept that avoidance urges last only so long. They are not terminal.

- Rather than waiting to feel inspired while lying on the couch, wait out your urge to diverge while riding your bicycle to the gym.

- Refuse to accept the thought that exercise is impossible to do if you are severely depressed or that it would be worthless even if you could do it. Instead, treat such thinking as hypothetical. Test your hypotheses, even in small measure (see Activities 5 and 25).

37: BOOST YOUR EMOTIONAL VOCABULARY

What to Know

It's hard to know what to do when all you feel is "bad." The more emotion words you have at your disposal, the better! Let's bone up your emotional vocabulary:

abandoned	dejected	mistrustful
accepting	demoralized	passionate
afraid	detached	peaceful
agitated	disappointed	prejudiced
amicable	empathic	restful
angry	frustrated	righteous
anxious	guilty	sad
apprehensive	harmonious	safer
ashamed	hostile	satisfied
benevolent	impatient	serene
blaming	irritable	skeptical
blissful	kind	suspicious
blue	laid back	tranquil
bored	let down	transcendent
calm	lonely	unconcerned
caring	loving	vengeful
compassionate	melancholy	victimized
connected	mellow	warmhearted

What to Do

The goal for the next three weeks is to learn and use three of the words from the list each day. To reach your goal, we recommend that you use each word at least one time to describe some type of direct experience you are having.

For example, you could pick the words "frustrated," "curious," and "shy" as the emotion words of the day. During the day, pay close attention to what you feel, think, and do, and try to use those words either together or separately to describe some type of experience you are having at work, at home, at school, or when you are on your own. If you follow this simple exercise, at the end of three weeks you will have used over sixty different words to describe and deal with stress-related emotions. This will make a huge difference in how you experience stress. You will notice a difference in how you understand and relate to emotions. This doesn't mean you won't have stress; it just means that you will be able to describe emotions more accurately and control urges to engage in escape or avoidance behaviors.

38: TAKE THE MIDDLE PATH

What to Know

This exercise invites you to identify an activity that you believe will support you in developing less reactivity and more balance in your day-to-day perspectives on life.

First, describe a recent emotionally triggering situation or event. Then, imagine what an overreaction to that event would look like. Next, report from the perspective of the middle path—describe just the facts in a nonreactive way without injecting or attaching to your judgments. Finally, think about a lifestyle activity that would act as a regular cue for you to practice taking the middle path. These types of activities may include becoming a part of a spiritual community, such as a church; joining a yoga or meditation group; or participating in a sports activity involving self-discipline and mental focus.

What to Do

Develop a plan to take the middle path when you are triggered to overreact, whether toward yourself or others. Practice by describing a challenging event, situation, or interation you're struggling with and then answering the following questions:

1. What would it look like if you overreacted?

2. What would it look like if you took the middle path?

3. What would help you adopt a middle-path perspective in your life?

What happened when you imagined taking the middle path instead of being emotionally reactive and judgmental? Did you feel the burden of suffering lift a little bit? Did you feel a sense that it might be easier to roll with this situation if you stayed focused on the middle path? By training yourself not to overreact to "small stuff," you can conserve a lot of your mental energy!

39: IDENTIFY POSITIVE EMOTION TARGETS

What to Know

Identifying positive emotion targets in different areas of life will let you diversify the ways that you induce positive emotions in your daily routine. Keep in mind that you don't have to choose something that will be done every day at the same time. You can vary the time, frequency, and type of activity as you like.

What to Do

Set a goal at the beginning of each day to experience a positive emotion from the list below and follow through:

- Awakening senses (for example, smelling a rose, eating an orange slowly, watching the sunset mindfully, belly breathing for five minutes)

- Gratitude (for example, thanking someone for doing something nice, spending some time with mental images of things you are grateful for in your life)

- Generosity (for example, opening a door for someone, buying a coworker a latte just to be nice)

- Connectedness (for example, going to church or a spiritual meeting, going to lunch with a friend, holding hands with your spouse while walking together)

- Compassion (for example, doing a five-minute compassion meditation, helping someone who needs help, forgiving yourself for a recent mistake you made— however small— and savoring it)

- Play (for example, taking kids to a playground or running around with them, going to a movie with your partner, getting into a tickling game with your partner or children)

- Valuing (for example, sitting down with your partner and sharing how you've been doing today, exercising for twenty to thirty minutes, preparing a healthy meal for everyone in the family)

How did you do at identifying positive emotion—generating actions that you could savor? When you imagined doing them, did you notice a feeling of positivity inside? If so, that's a good indicator that you're likely to experience positivity if you select that behavior. Were you able to figure out when would be the most convenient time to engage in an action? It's okay to fit these things around your existing lifestyle. Sometimes though, you have to prioritize between something you are used to doing and something you would like to be doing in your daily routine. Often, we are taught that it's only after we complete everything on our to-do list that we get to do something fun, relaxing, or introspective. Try not to get drawn into that trap; it's just your reactive mind giving you more rules to follow!

40: SUPER SLEEPING

What to Know

Most of us think of sleep as this big waste of time, when our brain doesn't do much. But in fact, sleep has an intricate architecture that is affected by our waking lives. And in a great example of an upward spiral, in which one positive change leads to other positive outcomes, the quality of our sleep affects in turn our quality of life.

The quality of your sleep is also affected by daily chemical fluctuations called circadian rhythms, which control a large number of processes, including hunger, alertness, and body temperature.

Sleep quality is best when your sleeping schedule is synchronized with your circadian rhythms. Unfortunately, there are many ways modern society can knock us out of that synchronization. The first is by looking at bright light at the wrong time. After the sun sets, your circadian rhythms tell your brain that it's nighttime and that it should start getting ready for sleep. But if you turn on bright lights, your brain thinks it's still daytime (after all, it evolved long before the lightbulb), and your circadian rhythms are shifted. Many light sources can shift the circadian cycle, including lamps, television screens, computers— even your cell phone.

If consistent, regular sleep is something you're struggling with, consider taking steps to improve your sleep hygiene. It'll probably improve your mood, too.

What to Do

- Avoid bright lights after the sun goes down. You don't need to walk around in the dark, but when it's getting close to bedtime, turn off most of the lights in your house. Turn down the brightness on your computer monitor or, better yet, don't stare at a screen at all. And make sure your bedroom is really dark when you're trying to sleep. If you've got several electronic devices in your bedroom that have LED lights, they can make enough light to disrupt your sleep. Move them to another room or cover the LEDs.

- Write down your worries. As we've discussed, worrying disrupts sleep because it activates the prefrontal cortex— and so does planning. If you're worrying or planning while trying to fall asleep, write down your thoughts. Get them out of your head and onto a piece of paper and be done with it.

- Make your environment comfortable. Quality sleep requires calming the brain, while being uncomfortable activates the brain's stress response. If your bedroom is too cold or hot, too bright, noisy, or even smelly, your sleep could be disrupted without your conscious awareness. So, do something about it. If there's noise you can't get rid of, add a white-noise maker like a fan, because that's less distracting to the brain.

- Brighten your day. Bright lights during the day help synchronize your circadian rhythms and improve your sleep.

So, take a few minutes to go walking in the sunshine. This has the added benefit of boosting your serotonin and reducing pain. One study on the effects of serotonin looked at patients recovering from spinal surgery in the hospital. Patients who were on the sunny side of the hospital had less stress and needed less pain medication (Walch et al. 2005). If you can't be near a window or go outside, at least try to work in a brightly lit environment while the sun is shining.

41: CREATE AN EMERGENCY PLAN

What to Know

When people feel very depressed, they cannot always think clearly. If you are not thinking clearly, you may not be able to take care of yourself the way that you need to. Creating an emergency plan while you are feeling good gives you an effective tool to keep yourself safe if you are ever not thinking clearly.

Take a look at Jordan's emotional emergency plan below.

Step 1: Stop thinking about whatever is making me feel depressed—right now. Put my mind on something that makes me feel good.

Step 2: Take a few deep breaths so I can help myself think clearly.

Step 3: Make a list of all the good things in my life, including everything I can think of.

Step 4: Remind myself of all the times I have gotten through hard situations in the past.

Step 5: Remind myself that this feeling is only temporary, and it will pass.

Step 6: Talk to my mom, my best friend, Lindsay, my Aunt Sarah, or my counselor, and tell them how I feel.

Once she'd drafted her plan, Jordan made four copies of it. Then, she put one in her office, one in her purse, and one in her night-table drawer, and she gave one to her mom. Once her plan was in place, she felt confident that she could get through a hard time with depression without hurting herself.

What to Do

Following the example, make a list of all the things that you know would help you come out of depression and all the people who could help you if you feel extremely depressed. (And see the resources list at the end of this book if you need ideas.) Write your own emotional emergency plan below. Make as many copies as you need and put them in places where they will be handy if you need them.

More to Do

- Think about what you know about yourself and how events in your life affect you. Write down any situations where you think an emotional emergency plan could be helpful for you.

- Share your answers with someone you trust. Talk about how you will act if any of these situations ever arise. Then, choose at least two other people to share your emergency plan with. Write their names and numbers on the emergency plan itself and explain to them why you chose them and what they might need to do.

- Sit quietly for a moment and close your eyes. Picture yourself at a time when you feel very depressed. Picture yourself taking out your emergency plan at that moment and one by one, putting the steps you have chosen into action. Picture yourself finding help and relief by using your plan. Picture yourself feeling better.

PART 5

DEAL WITH THE TOUGH STUFF

42: HANDLE SOCIAL REJECTION

What to Know

Whether you have depression or not, other people can often be a source of stress and anxiety. Our brains are wired to care what people think about us, which is why feeling judged or rejected is so distressing. In fact, as demonstrated in an experiment with fMRI technology—which measures brain activity to reveal which areas of the brain perform particular functions—social exclusion activates the same circuitry as physical pain (Eisenberger, Jarcho, Lieberman, and Naliboff 2006). So, we avoid social exclusion for the same reason we avoid touching a hot stove: it hurts!

Interestingly, people with low self-esteem appear to experience greater activation in the anterior cingulate (an area of the brain associated with emotions, especially sadness) than those with average or high self-esteem, suggesting their brains are more sensitive to social rejection (Onoda et al. 2010). And in depression, too, the brain tends to have greater sensitivity to social rejection, generating a stronger stress response. Now, increased sensitivity to social rejection is not inherently a bad thing. In fact, it's often what creates group harmony, because it makes people want to fit in. However, it puts you at risk for a downward spiral in those moments when someone seems to reject you—even when the rejection is not actually real, and it's your threat-sensitive brain that tells you it is.

When other people have the power to hurt you, it makes sense that you'd want to be alone sometimes. It's a perfectly reasonable coping mechanism and fine in moderation. But unfortunately, it can also be like eating ice cream to cope with stress in that it makes you feel better momentarily but doesn't actually solve the problem. Which is to say that when you're depressed, you want to keep a close eye on whether you're using alone time in a healthy way—to recuperate when you're especially overwhelmed and to make what you're dealing with more manageable for you—or if you're reacting defensively and excessively to what's actually not rejection, but misunderstanding.

What to Do

Reflect on rejection. We often experience something as rejection when it's really just a misunderstanding. For example, maybe you leave a message for a friend, and he or she doesn't call you back. It's easy to assume the intention was to hurt you or that your friend doesn't care enough about you. But those are not the only options. A more likely scenario is that your friend got too busy and forgot—or just missed the message in the first place. Thinking of alternate possibilities activates the medial prefrontal cortex—improving regulation over the limbic system (the part of the brain involved in behavioral or emotional responses) and helping you feel better. Sometimes asking the friend to clarify his or her intentions can be helpful. Furthermore, recognize that feelings of social rejection are enhanced by a bad mood or depression. So, however bad it seems, it's not really that bad.

43: MANAGE SEASONAL AFFECTIVE DISORDER

What to Know

Many people enjoy light, sunny days more than dark, cloudy days. But some people are so sensitive to the amount of light they receive that it can affect their moods to a stronger degree. People who become very depressed during the darker winter months may suffer from a condition called seasonal affective disorder (SAD). A milder form of this condition is called the "winter blues."

Exposure to light and dark has an effect on our bodies. Melatonin, a chemical related to sleep, is produced more when it's dark. Serotonin, a chemical related to feeling good, is produced more when it's light. During the winter months, when there is less sunlight, some people's bodies produce such a great amount of melatonin and such a small amount of serotonin that they can start to feel depressed. Symptoms of seasonal disorders can include depression, irritability, lack of energy, increased need for sleep, craving for sweets, overeating, weight gain, difficulty concentrating, and decrease of interest in social activities. These symptoms may begin as early as autumn, reach their peak in January and February, and decrease again in spring.

What to Do

If you experience symptoms of SAD or winter blues, you can help yourself in these ways:

- Educate yourself, your friends, and your family about these conditions.

- Try phototherapy, or "light therapy." Exposure to special bright-light boxes can reduce depressive symptoms in some people.

- Use higher-wattage bulbs or full-spectrum bulbs.

- Increase your exposure to outdoor light by spending more time outdoors, clearing windows and doors of heavy draperies, rearranging workspaces so that you spend more time near a window, or sitting next to windows in public places.

- Exercise on a regular basis, outdoors if possible, or indoors near a window.

- Ask for help with schoolwork if you have a hard time concentrating.

- Try to eat nutritiously to keep your energy level up and your health stable.

- Try to keep a stable sleep routine and remain awake during as many daylight hours as possible.

- Make it easier for yourself to awaken by putting your bedroom lights on a timer that turns on thirty minutes before you get up.

- Take a vacation to a warmer, sunnier climate, if possible.

- Talk to a counselor about your feelings and learn healthy ways to cope.

More to Do

Think about whether you are strongly affected by the change in sunlight throughout the year. For each category below, use a 1–5 scale to show how you are during the winter months, five meaning high amounts, or a lot:

- My energy level

- The amount I sleep

- My depression level

- My irritability level.

- How productive I am

- How hungry I am

- How much I eat

- How much I weigh

- How well I can concentrate

- How much I like to socialize

- How happy I am in general

Look back at your ratings and circle the categories you have rated 3 or lower. These are indications that the winter months are affecting your mood.

Go through some of the healthy coping strategies you learned earlier in the book. Tell yourself which of the coping ideas you think would best help you manage your seasonal feelings of depression.

44: REPAIR RIPS IN YOUR RELATIONSHIPS

What to Know

Sooner or later, practically everyone has relationship interference-provoking strains, or RIPS, for different reasons and in varied degrees. Some are temporary. Others linger. Depression is one of those conditions that can lead to lingering RIPS.

When one partner in a relationship is significantly depressed, this is likely to stress the other partner. However, interactions before and during depression may be similar. For example, bickering and fighting often characterize the interactions of couples in distressed relationships even if depression is not present (Jackman-Cram, Dobson, and Martin 2006). When RIPS occur in marital relations, these frictions may include further hostility and lack of affection, and a major depression may follow (Gotlib and Hammen 1992).

A deliberate effort to practice empathy with others and forge stronger connections with them can interfere with this destructive pattern. Awareness of potential RIPS opens an opportunity for you to suppress the urge to escalate and try a different, perhaps more empathic, way. Like most significant changes, it normally takes time and effort to tip the balance in your relationships from discord toward empathy—but you can do it if you try.

A client named Danny was in love with his wife. One morning he woke up and hated her. He got a divorce but then wondered if it was a mistake. Danny was prone to bipolar depression. His history showed a pattern of major life changes when his depression came out of the blue: changing jobs, moving to a new area, divorce.

Danny engaged in self-empathy. He accepted that his perceptions and thoughts get distorted when he is depressed. He helped stabilize his routines with activity scheduling. He worked to break his dysfunctional pattern by suspending judgments about any major changes when he was depressed. And he took steps to preserve his current relationships by following five E's:

- **Examine** your relationships to identify opportunities where you can create empathic bridges. For example, your depression may be more tenacious than you'd prefer, and you have to accept that it takes time to work your way out of depression. Knowing this can help you be empathic toward someone else who experiences frustration.

- **Evaluate** your opportunities to keep paths open between you and those who are normally significant to you. What three people are most important to you? What can you do to reach out constructively? For example, on special occasions, send a gift that fits with their hobby or interests. Set a date when lunch is on you. Drop them a quick email to see how they're doing.

- **Explain** to others that you appreciate their patience during your period of depression. Empathize with others' challenges, such as noting that you may not be so pleasant to be around when you are off-kilter with depression. If you have a support group, acknowledging their contribution in support of your well-being can make it easier for all parties to weather the storm.

- **Elicit** feedback from the people in your life as to how you can improve communication with them.

- **Evolve** your relationships. Stretch a bit. Entertain new ideas about how your connection with someone could change. Examine your personal limit for how far you might go to stay with someone, and try to linger at that limit zone. See how you feel pushing yourself to do something out of your comfort zone for someone else. In time, you may feel socially reconnected.

The E factors for empathy building will help you find a bridge between yourself and the people in your life—especially when your depression is making it hard for you to be the kind of partner, friend, coworker, and more that you want to be—so you can build the kind of relationships that can make depression easier to deal with.

What to Do

If there's a relationship in your life that's particularly stressed, use empathy in repairing those RIPS.

1. Examine the reasons for the RIPS.

2. Evaluate opportunities for making repairs.

3. Explain what you want to accomplish.

4. Elicit cooperation.

5. Evolve the relationship with joint problem solving.

Feel free to use a piece of paper to write down reflections and plan next steps.

45: COPE WITH CHANGE

What to Know

It's normal to experience some feelings of discomfort when you're faced with life events that bring about change, even when the change is positive. Adjusting to change, whatever its nature, takes time and energy. But when you can learn healthy ways to cope with change, discomfort will pass more quickly instead of turning into depression.

As long as you are alive, you will experience change. It's a normal part of being human. The world is designed to change; seasons change, weather changes, all living things grow and develop and change over the course of their lives.

While it's possible to adjust to change, it involves thinking and acting in new ways, which requires time and energy. When you are aware that you need this extra time and energy, you can understand that adjusting to change doesn't happen immediately. Although this may make you uncomfortable for a while, this feeling is normal and will pass. In the meantime, you can focus on helping yourself through the transition.

What to Do

Practicing any of the healthy coping actions below can help you through a time of change. Some preserve and create energy; some release depressive feelings, which require energy to hold inside:

- Getting enough sleep (creates energy)

- Eating healthy foods (creates energy)

- Getting fresh air (creates energy)

- Getting physical exercise (creates energy and releases depression)

- Expressing your feelings by talking or writing (releases depression)

- Focusing on the positive in yourself and the situation (releases depression)

- Reminding yourself things will eventually get better (releases depression)

- Participating in fun activities (releases depression)

- Laughing (creates energy and releases depression)

Choose a recent life event from your timeline. In a notebook or on a separate sheet of paper, describe how you used, or could have used, each of the coping actions to help yourself through it.

Event:

Sleep:

Healthy foods:

Fresh air:

Exercise:

Expression of feelings:

Focusing on the positives:

Thinking of what will it be like when things get better:

Fun activities:

Laughter:

Now, think of a life event that is coming up for you in the near future. Describe how you can use each of the coping actions outlined above to help yourself through this.

46: AVOID SELF-SOOTHING WITH SUBSTANCES

What to Know

Some people want so much to escape from their feelings of depression that they use mood-altering substances, such as alcohol or street drugs, to try to feel better quickly. Unfortunately, because of the way they affect the brain, these substances often end up making the depression worse. Instead of helping the problem, alcohol and street drugs only make the problem bigger.

When we try to self-medicate by using alcohol or drugs to make ourselves feel better, it can feel good at first. But eventually, you end up feeling worse than when you started. This is because repeated use of these substances damages brain receptors and the brain messengers known as neurotransmitters.

Neurotransmitters are chemicals that help in transmitting messages between nerve cells in the brain. Certain neurotransmitters regulate our moods. And again, alcohol and drugs can damage these neurotransmitters, which can make users feel depressed even when they weren't to begin with.

Alcohol and drug use can also contribute to depressing situations and behaviors, such as decreased school performance, problems with family and social relationships, poor concentration, and low energy levels. Being arrested for illegal use of alcohol or drugs also becomes a risk, and this is another life event that can contribute to depression. Ultimately, when it comes to depression and low mood, alcohol and drugs are often "quick fixes" that end up not being able to fix anything at all.

If substances have become a way you deal with your depression, and if your use has become a problem for you, it's worth trying to find alternatives to the quick fix substances represent—one that's more effective to soothe you and solve your problems.

What to Do

Think a situation where you tried to use a quick fix to solve a problem. Did the quick fix solve the problem permanently?

What would actually have been required to solve the problem permanently?

Describe a situation where a family member or friend tried to use a quick fix to solve a problem. Think if the quick fix solved the problem permanently.

What would actually have been required to solve the problem permanently?

Why do you think people try to use quick fixes if they know that these won't really solve problems permanently?

How can using alcohol or drugs make you end up feeling even more depressed?

APPENDIX: ADDITIONAL HELP AND SUPPORT RESOURCES

If you need a therapist, the following organization can help you find a therapist trained in cognitive behavioral therapy (CBT).

The Association for Behavioral & Cognitive Therapies (ABCT)
Find-a-Therapist service offers a list of therapists schooled in CBT techniques. Therapists listed are licensed professionals who have met the membership requirements of ABCT and who have chosen to appear in the directory.

Visit https://www.abct.org and click on Find a CBT Therapist or Find Help.

For support for patients, family, and friends, please contact the following:

Anxiety and Depression Association of American (ADAA)
Visit http://www.adaa.org.

Depression and Bipolar Support Alliance (DBSA)
Visit http://www.dbsalliance.org.

National Suicide Prevention Lifeline
Call the 24-hour hotline 1-800-273-TALK (8255) or visit http://www.suicidepreventionlifeline.org.

REFERENCES

Armitage, C. J., P. R. Harris, G. Hepton, and L. Napper. 2008. "Self-Affirmation Increases Acceptance of Health-Risk Information Among UK Adult Smokers with Low Socioeconomic Status." *Psychology of Addictive Behaviors* 22: 88–95.

Brown, F., W. Buboltz, and B. Soper. 2002. "Relationship of Sleep Hygiene Awareness, Sleep Hygiene Practices, and Sleep Quality in University Students." *Behavioral Medicine* 27: 33–38.

Eisenberger, N. I., J. M. Jarcho, M. D. Lieberman, and B. D. Naliboff. 2006. "An Experimental Study of Shared Sensitivity to Physical Pain and Social Rejection." *Pain* 126: 132–138.

Epley, N., J. Schroeder, and A. Waytz. 2013. "Motivated Mind Perception: Treating Pets as People and People as Animals." In S. J. Gervais (Ed.), *Objectification and (De)Humanization.* New York: Springer.

Epton, T., and P. R. Harris. 2008. "Self-Affirmation Promotes Health Behavior Change." *Health Psychology* 27: 746–752.

Field, T., M. Hernandez-Reif, M. Diego, S. Schanberg, and C. Kuhn. 2005. "Cortisol Decreases and Serotonin and Dopamine Increase Following Massage Therapy." *International Journal of Neuroscience* 115: 1397–1413.

Froh, J. J., C Yurkewicz, and T. B. Kashdan. 2009. "Gratitude and subjective well-being in early adolescence: Examining gender differences." *Journal of Adolescence* 32: 633–650.

Gotlib, I. H., and C. L. Hammen. 1992. *Psychological Aspects of Depression: Toward a Cognitive-Interpersonal Integration.* Oxford, England: John Wiley and Sons.

Heller, W., and J. B. Nitschke. 1997. "Regional Brain Activity in Emotion: A Framework for Understanding Cognition in Depression." *Cognition and Emotion* 11: 637–661.

Irwin, M., C. Miller, G. C. Gillin, A. Demodena, and C. L. Ehlers. 2000. "Polysomnograhic and Spectral Sleep EEG in Primary Alcoholics: An Interaction Between Alcohol Dependence and African-American Ethnicity." *Alcoholism Clinical and Experimental Research* 24: 1376–1384.

Jackman-Cram, S., K. S. Dobson, and R. Martin. 2006. Marital problem-solving behavior in depression and marital distress. *Journal of Abnormal Psychology* 115 (2): 380–384.

Joseph, N. T., H. F. Myers, J. R. Schettino, N. T. Olmos, C. Bingham-Mira, I. Lesser, et al. 2011. "Support and Undermining in Interpersonal Relationships Are Associated with Symptom Improvement in a Trial of Antidepressant Medication." *Psychiatry* 7: 240–254.

Leasure, J. L., and M. Jones. 2008. "Forced and Voluntary Exercise Differentially Affect Brain and Behavior." *Neuroscience* 156: 456–465.

Levenson, D., E. Stoll, S. Kindy, and R. Davidson. 2014. "A Mind You Can Count On: Validating Breath Counting as a Behavioral Measure of Mindfulness." *Frontiers of Psychology: Consciousness* 120: 1–10.

Lund, I., Y. Ge, L.-C. Yu, K., Unväs-Moberg, J. Wang, C. Yu, et al. 2002. "Repeated Massage-Like Stimulation Induces Long-Term Effects on Nociception: Contribution of Oxytocinergic Mechanisms." *European Journal of Neuroscience* 16: 330–338.

Nerbass, F. B., M. I. Feltrim, S. A. De Souza, D. S. Ykeda, and G. Lorenzi-Filho. 2010. "Effects of Massage Therapy on Sleep Quality After Coronary Artery Bypass Graft Surgery." *Clinics (Sao Paulo)* 65: 1105–1110.

Onoda, K., Y. Okamoto, K. Nakashima, H. Nittono, S. Yoshimura, S. Yamawaki, et al. 2010. "Does Low Self-Esteem Enhance Social

Pain? The Relationship Between Trait Self-Esteem and Anterior Cingulate Cortex Activation Induced by Ostracism." *Social Cognitive and Affective Neuroscience* 5: 385–391.

Pretty, J., J. Peacock, M. Sellens, and M. Griffin. 2005. "The Mental and Physical Health Outcomes of Green Exercise." *International Journal of Environmental Health Research* 15: 319–337.

Roehrs, T., and T. Roth. 2001. "Sleep, Sleepiness, Sleep Disorders and Alcohol Use and Abuse." *Sleep Medicine Reviews* 5: 287–297.

Reid, K. J., K. G. Baron, B. Lu, E. Naylor, L. Wolfe, and P. C. Zee. 2010. "Aerobic Exercise Improves Self-Reported Sleep and Quality of Life in Older Adults with Insomnia." *Sleep Medicine* 11: 934–940.

Sayal, K., S. Checkley, M. Rees, C. Jacobs, T. Harris, A. Papadopoulos, et al. 2002. "Effects of Social Support During Weekend Leave on Cortisol and Depression Ratings: A Pilot Study." *Journal of Affective Disorders* 71: 153–157.

Tops, M., Riese, H., Oldehinkel, A. J., Rijsdijke, F. V., & Ormel, J. (2008). Rejection sensitivity relates to hypocortisolism and depressed mood state in young women. *Psychoneuroendocrinology, 33(5)*: 551–559.

Uvnäs-Moberg, K. 1998. "Oxytocin May Mediate the Benefits of Positive Social Interaction and Emotions." *Psychoneuroendocrinology* 23: 819–835.

Walch, J. M., B. S. Rabin, R. Day, J. N. Williams, K. Choi, and J. D. Kang. 2005. "The Effect of Sunlight on Postoperative Analgesic Medication Use: A Prospective Study of Patients Undergoing Spinal Surgery." *Psychosomatic Medicine* 67: 156–163.

William J. Knaus, EdD, is a licensed psychologist with more than forty-six years of clinical experience working with people suffering from anxiety, depression, and procrastination. He has appeared on numerous regional and national television shows, including *The Today Show*, and more than one hundred radio shows. His ideas have appeared in national magazines such as *U.S. News & World Report* and *Good Housekeeping*, and major newspapers such as *The Washington Post* and *Chicago Tribune*. He is one of the original directors of postdoctoral psychotherapy training in rational emotive behavior therapy (REBT). Knaus is author or coauthor of more than twenty-five books, including *The Cognitive Behavioral Workbook for Anxiety*, *The Cognitive Behavioral Workbook for Depression*, and *The Procrastination Workbook*.

Alex Korb, PhD, is a neuroscientist, writer, and coach. He has studied the brain and mental health for more than fifteen years, starting with an undergraduate degree in neuroscience from Brown University; before earning a PhD in neuroscience from the University of California, Los Angeles (UCLA). He is author of *The Upward Spiral* and *The Upward Spiral Workbook*, and is currently adjunct assistant professor at UCLA in the department of psychiatry and biobehavioral sciences. Outside of the lab, he is available for personal coaching, consulting services, and speaking engagements. He is head coach of the UCLA Women's Ultimate Frisbee team, and has a wealth of experience in yoga and mindfulness, physical fitness, and even stand-up comedy.

Patricia J. Robinson, PhD, is director of training and program evaluation at Mountainview Consulting Group, Inc., a firm that assists health care systems with integrating behavioral health services into primary care settings. She is coauthor of *Real Behavior Change in Primary Care* and *The Mindfulness and Acceptance Workbook for Depression*. After exploring primary care psychology as a researcher, she devoted her efforts to its dissemination in rural America, urban public health departments, and military medical treatment facilities.

Lisa M. Schab, LCSW, is a practicing psychotherapist in the greater Chicago, IL, area; and author of several self-help books, including *The Anxiety Workbook for Teens* and *The Self-Esteem Workbook for Teens*, as well as the teen guided journals, *Put Your Worries Here* and *Put Your Feelings Here*. She has been interviewed as an expert on the Milwaukee television stations WTMJ-TV and WISN-TV, and for articles in *The New York Times*, Scholastic's *Choices* magazine, *Teen Vogue*, *Psych Central*, and *Your Teen Magazine*. Schab has authored regular columns on tweens and teens for *Chicago Parent*, and on healthy families for The Sun Newspapers. She is a member of the National Association of Social Workers (NASW).

Kirk D. Strosahl, PhD, is cofounder of acceptance and commitment therapy (ACT), a cognitive behavioral approach that has gained widespread adoption in the mental health and substance abuse communities. He is coauthor of *Brief Interventions for Radical Change* and *In This Moment*. Strosahl provides training and consultation services for Mountainview Consulting Group, Inc. He is a pioneer in the movement to bring behavioral health services into primary care.

Real change *is* possible

For more than forty-five years, New Harbinger has published proven-effective self-help books and pioneering workbooks to help readers of all ages and backgrounds improve mental health and well-being, and achieve lasting personal growth. In addition, our spirituality books offer profound guidance for deepening awareness and cultivating healing, self-discovery, and fulfillment.

Founded by psychologist Matthew McKay and Patrick Fanning, New Harbinger is proud to be an independent, employee-owned company. Our books reflect our core values of integrity, innovation, commitment, sustainability, compassion, and trust. Written by leaders in the field and recommended by therapists worldwide, New Harbinger books are practical, accessible, and provide real tools for real change.

newharbingerpublications

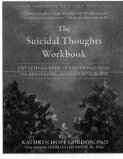

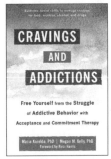